43 Russian Morning Meals Recipes for Home

By: Kelly Johnson

Table of Contents

- Blini (Russian Pancakes)
- Syrniki (Russian Cheese Pancakes)
- Oladi (Russian Mini Pancakes)
- Kasha (Russian Porridge)
- Grechnevaya kasha (Buckwheat Porridge)
- Zapekanka (Baked Cottage Cheese Casserole)
- Pelmeni (Russian Dumplings)
- Pirozhki (Stuffed Buns)
- Borscht (Beet Soup)
- Okroshka (Cold Summer Soup)
- Olivier Salad (Russian Potato Salad)
- Mimosa Salad (Layered Salad with Fish)
- Herring Under a Fur Coat (Layered Herring Salad)
- Selyodka Pod Shuboy (Herring Under a Fur Coat)
- Zakuski (Russian Appetizers)
- Khachapuri (Georgian Cheese Bread)
- Chakhokhbili (Georgian Chicken Stew)
- Khinkali (Georgian Dumplings)
- Lobio (Georgian Bean Stew)
- Adjaruli Khachapuri (Georgian Cheese Bread with Egg)
- Kubdari (Georgian Meat Pie)
- Mtsvadi (Georgian Shish Kebabs)
- Pkhali (Georgian Vegetable Pâté)
- Ajapsandali (Georgian Vegetable Stew)
- Churchkhela (Georgian Candy)
- Lobiani (Georgian Bean-Stuffed Bread)
- Badrijani Nigvzit (Georgian Eggplant Rolls)
- Satsivi (Georgian Chicken in Walnut Sauce)
- Chashushuli (Georgian Beef Stew)
- Kharcho (Georgian Beef Soup)
- Jonjoli (Georgian Pickled Flowers)
- Kupati (Georgian Sausages)
- Mchadi (Georgian Cornbread)
- Acharuli Khachapuri (Georgian Cheese Bread with Egg)
- Satsivi (Georgian Chicken in Walnut Sauce)
- Pkhali (Georgian Vegetable Pâté)

- Khachapuri (Georgian Cheese Bread)
- Khinkali (Georgian Dumplings)
- Ostri (Georgian Beef Stew)
- Chashushuli (Georgian Beef Stew)
- Khinkali (Georgian Dumplings)
- Lobio (Georgian Bean Stew)
- Ajapsandali

Blini (Russian Pancakes)

Ingredients:

- 1 cup all-purpose flour
- 1 cup milk
- 2 large eggs
- 1 tablespoon melted butter (plus more for cooking)
- 1/4 teaspoon salt
- 1/2 teaspoon sugar (optional, for sweet blini)
- Additional butter or oil for cooking

Instructions:

1. **Prepare the batter:**
   - In a large mixing bowl, whisk together the flour, salt, and sugar (if using).
   - In a separate bowl, whisk together the milk, eggs, and melted butter until well combined.
2. **Combine wet and dry ingredients:**
   - Gradually pour the wet ingredients into the dry ingredients, whisking constantly to avoid lumps. Continue whisking until the batter is smooth and thin. It should have the consistency of heavy cream.
3. **Rest the batter:**
   - Let the batter rest at room temperature for at least 30 minutes. This allows the flour to fully hydrate and ensures tender blini.
4. **Cook the blini:**
   - Heat a non-stick skillet or griddle over medium heat. Brush the surface lightly with melted butter or oil.
   - Pour a small ladleful (about 1/4 cup) of batter onto the skillet and quickly swirl it around to spread it thinly and evenly.
5. **Cook until golden:**
   - Cook the blini for about 1-2 minutes on the first side, until the edges start to lift and the bottom is golden brown. Use a spatula to flip the blini and cook for another 1-2 minutes on the second side.
6. **Stack and keep warm:**
   - Remove the cooked blini from the skillet and stack them on a plate. Cover with a clean kitchen towel to keep them warm while you cook the remaining batter.
7. **Serve:**
   - Serve blini warm, traditionally folded or rolled, with your choice of toppings or fillings.

Serving Suggestions:

- **Sweet toppings:** Sour cream, jam, honey, fresh berries, or sweetened condensed milk.

- **Savory fillings:** Smoked salmon, sour cream, caviar, sautéed mushrooms, cheese, or meats.

Tips for Perfect Blini:

- **Consistency:** The batter should be thin enough to spread easily in the pan but not so thin that it tears.
- **Temperature:** Adjust the heat as needed to ensure the blini cook evenly without burning.
- **Storage:** Cooked blini can be stored in an airtight container in the refrigerator for a day or two. Reheat gently in a skillet or microwave before serving.

Blini are a delightful treat that can be enjoyed for breakfast, brunch, or as a snack. Experiment with different toppings and fillings to create your favorite Russian pancake variations!

Syrniki (Russian Cheese Pancakes)

Ingredients:

- 1 cup quark cheese or farmer's cheese (if unavailable, ricotta can be used)
- 1 egg
- 2-3 tablespoons sugar (adjust to taste)
- 1/2 teaspoon vanilla extract (optional)
- 1/4 teaspoon salt
- 1/2 cup all-purpose flour (plus more for dusting)
- 1/2 teaspoon baking powder
- Oil or butter, for frying
- Sour cream, jam, honey, or fresh berries, for serving

Instructions:

1. **Prepare the cheese:**
   - If using quark or farmer's cheese, place it in a mixing bowl. If using ricotta, drain any excess liquid first.
2. **Combine ingredients:**
   - To the cheese, add the egg, sugar, vanilla extract (if using), and salt. Mix well until smooth and creamy.
3. **Add dry ingredients:**
   - Sift the flour and baking powder into the cheese mixture. Stir until just combined. The dough should be soft and slightly sticky.
4. **Form the syrniki:**
   - Dust your hands with flour to prevent sticking. Take a spoonful of the dough and shape it into a ball. Flatten slightly to form a small pancake or patty. Repeat with the remaining dough.
5. **Fry the syrniki:**

- Heat a non-stick skillet or frying pan over medium heat. Add a small amount of oil or butter to coat the bottom of the pan.
- Place the syrniki in the skillet, leaving space between each pancake. Cook for about 3-4 minutes on each side, or until golden brown and cooked through.

6. **Serve:**
   - Transfer the cooked syrniki to a plate lined with paper towels to absorb excess oil. Serve warm with sour cream, jam, honey, or fresh berries.

Tips for Making Syrniki:

- **Cheese:** Quark or farmer's cheese is traditional for syrniki, providing a slightly tangy flavor. If using ricotta, ensure it's well drained to prevent excess moisture.
- **Flour:** Use just enough flour to bind the dough. Too much flour can make the syrniki dense.
- **Frying:** Fry syrniki over medium heat to ensure they cook through without burning. Adjust the heat as needed.
- **Variations:** Add raisins, chopped nuts, or cinnamon to the dough for extra flavor.

Syrniki are best enjoyed fresh and warm, making them a delightful treat for breakfast or brunch. Their crispy exterior and soft interior, paired with creamy toppings or fruity jams, create a delicious and comforting dish.

Oladi (Russian Mini Pancakes)

Ingredients:

- 1 cup all-purpose flour
- 1 cup kefir (or buttermilk)
- 1 large egg
- 2 tablespoons sugar
- 1/2 teaspoon baking soda
- 1/2 teaspoon salt
- Butter or oil, for frying
- Sour cream, jam, honey, fresh berries, or powdered sugar, for serving

Instructions:

1. **Prepare the batter:**
   - In a mixing bowl, whisk together the flour, sugar, baking soda, and salt until well combined.
2. **Add wet ingredients:**
   - In another bowl, beat the egg lightly, then add the kefir (or buttermilk) and mix until smooth.
3. **Combine wet and dry ingredients:**

- Pour the wet ingredients into the dry ingredients and stir until just combined. The batter should be thick but pourable. If it's too thick, you can add a little more kefir or buttermilk.
4. **Rest the batter:**
    - Let the batter rest for about 10-15 minutes at room temperature. This allows the baking soda to activate and helps the pancakes to rise.
5. **Heat the skillet:**
    - Heat a non-stick skillet or griddle over medium heat. Add a small amount of butter or oil and spread it evenly across the surface.
6. **Cook the oladi:**
    - Spoon about 1-2 tablespoons of batter for each pancake onto the skillet, leaving space between them. You can make the oladi as small or large as you prefer.
7. **Cook until golden brown:**
    - Cook the oladi for 2-3 minutes on the first side, or until bubbles start to form on the surface and the edges look set.
8. **Flip and cook the other side:**
    - Carefully flip the oladi with a spatula and cook for another 1-2 minutes on the other side, until golden brown and cooked through.
9. **Serve warm:**
    - Transfer the cooked oladi to a plate and cover with a kitchen towel to keep warm while you cook the remaining batter.
10. **Serve with toppings:**
    - Serve oladi warm with your choice of toppings such as sour cream, jam, honey, fresh berries, or a dusting of powdered sugar.

Tips for Making Oladi:

- **Consistency:** Adjust the thickness of the batter with more kefir/buttermilk if needed. It should be thick enough to hold its shape but still spread slightly on the skillet.
- **Flavor variations:** Add vanilla extract or lemon zest to the batter for extra flavor. You can also fold in blueberries or chocolate chips for a different twist.
- **Keep warm:** To keep oladi warm before serving, place them in a single layer on a baking sheet in a warm oven (about 200°F or 90°C) until ready to serve.

Oladi are a comforting and delicious treat that can be enjoyed for breakfast, brunch, or even as a snack. Their fluffy texture and versatility make them a favorite in Russian cuisine.

Kasha (Russian Porridge)

Ingredients:

- 1 cup buckwheat groats
- 2 cups water or broth (for savory kasha)
- Salt, to taste
- Butter or vegetable oil, for serving (optional)

- Sour cream, milk, or honey, for serving (optional)

Instructions:

1. **Rinse the buckwheat groats:**
   - Place the buckwheat groats in a fine-mesh sieve and rinse under cold water until the water runs clear. This helps remove excess starch and any debris.
2. **Toast the buckwheat groats (optional):**
   - In a dry skillet over medium heat, toast the rinsed buckwheat groats for about 3-5 minutes, stirring constantly, until they are lightly toasted and fragrant. Toasting enhances the nutty flavor of the buckwheat.
3. **Cook the buckwheat groats:**
   - In a medium saucepan, bring 2 cups of water or broth to a boil.
   - Add the toasted buckwheat groats to the boiling water.
   - Reduce the heat to low, cover the saucepan with a lid, and simmer for about 15-20 minutes, or until the buckwheat is tender and has absorbed most of the liquid. Stir occasionally to prevent sticking.
4. **Season and serve:**
   - Once the buckwheat is cooked, season with salt to taste.
   - Serve hot, optionally with a knob of butter or a drizzle of vegetable oil for added richness.
   - Traditionally, buckwheat kasha is served with a dollop of sour cream or a splash of milk. Honey can also be used for a touch of sweetness.

Tips for Making Buckwheat Kasha:

- **Variations:** Buckwheat kasha can be made sweet or savory. For a sweet version, you can cook it in milk instead of water/broth and add sugar, cinnamon, or other sweet spices. For a savory version, consider adding sautéed onions or mushrooms.
- **Storage:** Leftover buckwheat kasha can be stored in an airtight container in the refrigerator for up to 3 days. Reheat gently on the stovetop or in the microwave with a splash of water or broth to loosen it up.
- **Nutritional Benefits:** Buckwheat is a nutritious whole grain that is gluten-free and rich in fiber, protein, and minerals. It makes for a hearty and satisfying breakfast or side dish.

Buckwheat kasha is a comforting dish with a nutty flavor and fluffy texture, enjoyed across Russia and beyond. It's a versatile dish that can be adapted to various tastes and preferences, making it a staple in many households.

Grechnevaya kasha (Buckwheat Porridge)

Ingredients:

- 1 cup buckwheat groats
- 2 cups water or broth (for savory kasha)

- Salt, to taste
- Butter or vegetable oil, for serving (optional)
- Sour cream, milk, honey, or jam, for serving (optional)

Instructions:

1. **Prepare the buckwheat groats:**
   - Rinse the buckwheat groats under cold water in a fine-mesh sieve until the water runs clear. This helps remove excess starch and ensures a cleaner flavor.
2. **Toast the buckwheat groats (optional):**
   - In a dry skillet over medium heat, toast the rinsed buckwheat groats for about 3-5 minutes, stirring constantly, until they are lightly toasted and fragrant. Toasting enhances the nutty flavor of the buckwheat.
3. **Cook the buckwheat groats:**
   - In a medium saucepan, bring 2 cups of water or broth to a boil.
   - Add the toasted buckwheat groats to the boiling water.
   - Reduce the heat to low, cover the saucepan with a lid, and simmer for about 15-20 minutes, or until the buckwheat is tender and has absorbed most of the liquid. Stir occasionally to prevent sticking.
4. **Season and serve:**
   - Once the buckwheat is cooked, season with salt to taste.
   - Serve hot, optionally with a knob of butter or a drizzle of vegetable oil for added richness.
   - Buckwheat porridge is traditionally served with a dollop of sour cream, a splash of milk, honey, or even jam, depending on personal preference.

Tips for Making Grechnevaya Kasha:

- **Variations:** Buckwheat porridge can be made sweet or savory. For a sweet version, cook it in milk instead of water/broth and add sugar, cinnamon, or vanilla. For a savory version, consider adding sautéed onions or mushrooms during cooking.
- **Nutritional Benefits:** Buckwheat is highly nutritious, being rich in fiber, protein, and essential minerals such as manganese, magnesium, and iron. It is also low in fat and has a low glycemic index.
- **Storage:** Leftover buckwheat porridge can be stored in an airtight container in the refrigerator for up to 3 days. Reheat gently on the stovetop or in the microwave with a splash of water or milk to maintain its creamy consistency.

Grechnevaya kasha is not only a staple in Russian households but also a comforting and versatile dish that can be enjoyed for breakfast, lunch, or dinner. Its nutty flavor and satisfying texture make it a favorite among those looking for wholesome and filling meal options.

Zapekanka (Baked Cottage Cheese Casserole)

Ingredients:

- 500g cottage cheese (about 2 cups)
- 2 large eggs
- 1/4 cup sugar (adjust to taste)
- 1/4 cup semolina (or farina, cream of wheat)
- 1/2 teaspoon vanilla extract
- Zest of 1 lemon (optional)
- 1/2 cup raisins (optional)
- Butter or oil, for greasing the baking dish
- Sour cream or jam, for serving (optional)

Instructions:

1. **Preheat the oven:** Preheat your oven to 350°F (175°C). Grease a baking dish (about 8x8 inches or equivalent size) with butter or oil.
2. **Prepare the cottage cheese mixture:**
   - In a large mixing bowl, combine the cottage cheese, eggs, sugar, semolina, vanilla extract, lemon zest (if using), and raisins (if using). Mix well until all ingredients are evenly incorporated.
3. **Bake the zapekanka:**
   - Transfer the mixture into the greased baking dish, spreading it evenly with a spatula.
   - Bake in the preheated oven for about 35-45 minutes, or until the top is golden brown and the casserole is set. The exact baking time may vary depending on your oven and the thickness of the mixture.
4. **Serve:** Remove from the oven and let it cool slightly before slicing into squares or wedges.
   - Serve warm or at room temperature.
   - Optionally, serve with a dollop of sour cream or a spoonful of your favorite jam.

Tips for Making Zapekanka:

- **Variations:** You can add other ingredients such as dried fruits (like apricots or cherries), nuts (like chopped almonds or walnuts), or even chocolate chips for a sweeter version.
- **Semolina substitution:** If you don't have semolina or farina, you can use cream of wheat or even ground oats as a substitute.
- **Storage:** Zapekanka can be stored in an airtight container in the refrigerator for up to 3 days. Reheat gently in the oven or microwave before serving.
- **Texture preferences:** Some prefer a smoother texture, so you can blend the cottage cheese mixture in a food processor before baking. Others enjoy a more textured casserole, so mixing by hand is sufficient.

Zapekanka is a versatile dish that can be enjoyed for breakfast, dessert, or even as a snack. Its creamy texture and mildly sweet flavor make it a favorite among both children and adults.

Pelmeni (Russian Dumplings)

Ingredients:

For the dough:

- 2 cups all-purpose flour
- 1/2 teaspoon salt
- 1 large egg
- 1/2 cup water, or as needed

For the filling:

- 1/2 lb ground pork
- 1/2 lb ground beef
- 1 small onion, finely chopped
- 1 clove garlic, minced
- Salt and pepper, to taste

For serving (optional):

- Sour cream
- Vinegar
- Butter

Instructions:

1. **Make the dough:**
    - In a large mixing bowl, combine the flour and salt. Make a well in the center and add the egg and water.
    - Mix together until a dough forms. If the dough is too dry, add a bit more water, 1 tablespoon at a time, until it comes together.
    - Knead the dough on a floured surface for about 5-7 minutes, or until smooth and elastic. Cover with a damp cloth and let it rest for 30 minutes.
2. **Prepare the filling:**
    - In another bowl, combine the ground pork, ground beef, chopped onion, minced garlic, salt, and pepper. Mix well until all ingredients are evenly incorporated.
3. **Assemble the pelmeni:**
    - Roll out the dough on a floured surface until it is about 1/8 inch thick.
    - Use a round cookie cutter or the rim of a glass to cut out circles of dough, about 2 inches in diameter.
    - Place a small spoonful of the meat filling in the center of each dough circle.

4. **Shape the pelmeni:**
   - Fold the dough over the filling to form a half-moon shape. Pinch the edges together firmly to seal. You can also press the edges with a fork for a decorative pattern.
5. **Boil the pelmeni:**
   - Bring a large pot of salted water to a boil.
   - Carefully drop the pelmeni into the boiling water, a few at a time, stirring gently to prevent sticking.
   - Cook for about 5-7 minutes, or until the pelmeni float to the surface and are cooked through.
6. **Serve:**
   - Remove the cooked pelmeni with a slotted spoon and place them into serving bowls.
   - Serve hot with sour cream, vinegar, and melted butter on the side for dipping or drizzling, according to personal preference.

Tips for Making Pelmeni:

- **Freezing:** Pelmeni can be frozen before or after boiling. Place them on a baking sheet lined with parchment paper and freeze until solid, then transfer to a freezer bag or container. When ready to cook, boil frozen pelmeni without thawing, adding a few extra minutes to the cooking time.
- **Variations:** Some recipes include a mixture of meats, such as pork and beef, while others use only one type of meat. You can also add additional seasonings like herbs (such as dill or parsley) or spices (such as paprika or nutmeg) to the filling.
- **Dough consistency:** The dough should be smooth and elastic but not sticky. Adjust the amount of water or flour as needed to achieve the right texture.

Pelmeni are a delicious and comforting dish enjoyed across Russia and neighboring countries. They are perfect for sharing with family and friends, whether as a main course or a hearty appetizer.

Pirozhki (Stuffed Buns)

Dough Ingredients:

- 2 cups all-purpose flour
- 1 teaspoon sugar
- 1/2 teaspoon salt
- 1/2 cup warm milk
- 1/4 cup warm water
- 1 packet (2 1/4 teaspoons) active dry yeast
- 2 tablespoons vegetable oil
- 1 egg, beaten (for egg wash)

Meat Filling Ingredients:

- 1/2 lb ground beef or pork (or a mixture)
- 1 small onion, finely chopped
- 1 clove garlic, minced
- 1 tablespoon vegetable oil
- Salt and pepper, to taste
- Optional: herbs (such as dill or parsley), spices (such as paprika or cumin)

Instructions:

1. Prepare the Dough:

1. In a small bowl, combine the warm water, sugar, and yeast. Let it sit for about 5-10 minutes until foamy.
2. In a large mixing bowl, combine the flour and salt. Make a well in the center and add the yeast mixture, warm milk, and vegetable oil.
3. Mix until a dough forms. Knead the dough on a floured surface for about 5-7 minutes, or until it becomes smooth and elastic.
4. Place the dough in a lightly oiled bowl, cover with a damp cloth or plastic wrap, and let it rise in a warm place for about 1 hour, or until doubled in size.

2. Make the Meat Filling:

1. Heat vegetable oil in a skillet over medium heat. Add the chopped onion and garlic, and sauté until softened and translucent.
2. Add the ground meat to the skillet and cook until browned, breaking it up with a spoon as it cooks.
3. Season with salt, pepper, and any optional herbs or spices. Remove from heat and let it cool slightly.

3. Assemble the Pirozhki:

1. Preheat the oven to 375°F (190°C). Line a baking sheet with parchment paper.
2. Punch down the risen dough and divide it into equal-sized portions, about the size of a golf ball.
3. Roll each portion into a circle or oval shape on a lightly floured surface, about 1/4 inch thick.
4. Place a spoonful of the meat filling in the center of each dough circle. Fold the dough over the filling to form a half-moon shape. Pinch the edges together firmly to seal, or twist and fold the edges for a decorative pattern.
5. Place the filled pirozhki on the prepared baking sheet. Brush the tops with beaten egg for a shiny finish.

4. Bake the Pirozhki:

1. Bake in the preheated oven for about 20-25 minutes, or until the pirozhki are golden brown and cooked through.
2. Remove from the oven and let them cool slightly on a wire rack before serving.

5. Serve and Enjoy:

- Pirozhki can be served warm or at room temperature. They are delicious on their own or with a side of sour cream, ketchup, or a favorite dipping sauce.

Tips for Making Pirozhki:

- **Variations:** Besides meat fillings, pirozhki can be filled with mashed potatoes, cabbage, mushrooms, or even sweet fillings like jam or fruit.
- **Freezing:** You can freeze unbaked pirozhki on a baking sheet until solid, then transfer them to a freezer bag or container. Bake directly from frozen, adding a few extra minutes to the baking time.
- **Storage:** Leftover pirozhki can be stored in an airtight container in the refrigerator for up to 3 days. Reheat gently in the oven or microwave before serving.

Pirozhki are a versatile and comforting treat that can be enjoyed any time of day. Whether you prefer them baked or fried, savory or sweet, they are sure to be a hit at your table!

Borscht (Beet Soup)

Ingredients:

- 2 tablespoons vegetable oil
- 1 onion, finely chopped
- 2 carrots, peeled and grated
- 2-3 medium beets, peeled and grated
- 2 potatoes, peeled and diced
- 4 cups beef or vegetable broth
- 2 cups water
- 1 can (14 oz) diced tomatoes, with juice
- 1 tablespoon tomato paste
- 1 bay leaf
- 1 teaspoon sugar
- 2 cloves garlic, minced
- Salt and pepper, to taste
- 1 tablespoon vinegar (apple cider or white wine vinegar)
- Sour cream and fresh dill, for serving

Instructions:

1. **Prepare the Vegetables:**

- Heat vegetable oil in a large pot over medium heat. Add the chopped onion and grated carrots. Sauté for about 5 minutes, until softened.
2. **Add Beets and Potatoes:**
    - Add the grated beets and diced potatoes to the pot. Cook for another 5 minutes, stirring occasionally.
3. **Add Broth and Simmer:**
    - Pour in the beef or vegetable broth and water. Add the diced tomatoes (with their juice), tomato paste, bay leaf, sugar, minced garlic, salt, and pepper. Stir well to combine.
4. **Simmer the Soup:**
    - Bring the soup to a boil, then reduce the heat to low. Cover and simmer for about 30-40 minutes, or until the vegetables are tender.
5. **Add Vinegar:**
    - Stir in the vinegar. Taste and adjust seasoning with more salt, pepper, or sugar if needed. Remove the bay leaf.
6. **Serve:**
    - Ladle the borscht into bowls. Serve hot, topped with a dollop of sour cream and a sprinkle of fresh dill.

Tips for Making Borscht:

- **Beet Preparation:** Grating the beets ensures they cook quickly and evenly. Be careful, as beets can stain hands and surfaces.
- **Variations:** Borscht can be made with or without meat. Traditional versions often include beef or pork, but you can make a vegetarian version by using vegetable broth and omitting the meat.
- **Storage:** Borscht improves in flavor when allowed to sit for a day. Store leftovers in the refrigerator in an airtight container for up to 3 days.
- **Serving Suggestions:** Borscht is typically served with dark rye bread and additional sour cream on the side. Some also enjoy it with boiled potatoes on the side for a heartier meal.

Borscht is not only delicious but also nutritious, thanks to the abundance of vegetables and wholesome ingredients. It's a comforting soup that warms both the body and soul, making it a favorite in many households, especially during colder months.

Okroshka (Cold Summer Soup)

Ingredients:

- 2 cups kefir (Russian fermented milk drink) or buttermilk
- 1 cup plain yogurt
- 2 cups cold water
- 2-3 medium potatoes, boiled and diced
- 2 hard-boiled eggs, diced

- 1 cucumber, peeled and diced
- 1/2 bunch radishes, diced
- 1/4 cup fresh dill, chopped
- 1/4 cup fresh parsley, chopped
- 1/4 cup green onions, chopped
- 1 tablespoon mustard (optional)
- 1 tablespoon vinegar (white wine or apple cider)
- Salt and pepper, to taste
- Ice cubes, for serving

Instructions:

1. **Prepare the Vegetables:**
   - Peel and dice the boiled potatoes and hard-boiled eggs.
   - Peel and dice the cucumber.
   - Wash and dice the radishes. Chop the fresh dill, parsley, and green onions.
2. **Mix the Liquid Base:**
   - In a large bowl, combine the kefir (or buttermilk) and plain yogurt. Whisk until smooth.
   - Gradually add cold water to the mixture, stirring until well combined. The consistency should be thin but creamy.
3. **Season the Base:**
   - Stir in the mustard (if using) and vinegar. Season with salt and pepper to taste. Adjust the tartness with more vinegar if desired.
4. **Combine Ingredients:**
   - Add the diced potatoes, hard-boiled eggs, cucumber, radishes, fresh dill, parsley, and green onions to the liquid base. Mix gently to combine.
5. **Chill and Serve:**
   - Refrigerate the okroshka for at least 1 hour to chill thoroughly.
   - Serve cold, garnished with ice cubes for extra chillness, and additional fresh herbs if desired.

Tips for Making Okroshka:

- **Vegetable Variations:** Okroshka can include other vegetables like bell peppers, tomatoes, or celery. Feel free to customize according to your taste and seasonal availability.
- **Dairy Options:** Kefir and yogurt provide a tangy base, but you can adjust the ratio based on personal preference. Some recipes also use sour cream or a combination of sour cream and mayo.
- **Additional Flavorings:** Some variations include adding horseradish, lemon juice, or even kvass (a fermented beverage) for extra depth of flavor.
- **Make Ahead:** Okroshka can be prepared several hours in advance and stored in the refrigerator until ready to serve. The flavors meld together nicely over time.

Okroshka is a delightful dish that combines the freshness of summer vegetables with the coolness of a creamy base, making it a perfect dish to enjoy on a hot day. It's versatile, light, and packed with nutrients, making it a favorite in Russian cuisine during the summer months.

Olivier Salad (Russian Potato Salad)

Ingredients:

- 3-4 medium potatoes, boiled and diced
- 3-4 medium carrots, boiled and diced
- 3-4 large eggs, hard-boiled and diced
- 1 cup boiled peas (fresh or frozen)
- 1 cup diced dill pickles (or cornichons)
- 1/2 cup diced cooked ham or bologna (optional)
- 1/2 cup diced cooked chicken or beef (optional)
- 1/2 cup diced apples (optional, for a sweeter twist)
- 1/2 cup mayonnaise (plus more to taste)
- 2 tablespoons sour cream (optional, for a tangier dressing)
- 1 tablespoon Dijon mustard (optional, for a bit of tang)
- Salt and pepper, to taste
- Fresh dill, chopped, for garnish

Instructions:

1. **Prepare the Ingredients:**
   - Boil the potatoes and carrots until tender. Cool, peel, and dice into small cubes.
   - Boil the eggs until hard-boiled, cool, peel, and dice.
   - If using peas, boil or steam them until tender. Drain and let cool.
2. **Assemble the Salad:**
   - In a large mixing bowl, combine the diced potatoes, carrots, eggs, peas, dill pickles, and any optional ingredients (ham, chicken, beef, apples) if using.
3. **Make the Dressing:**
   - In a small bowl, mix together mayonnaise, sour cream (if using), and Dijon mustard (if using). Adjust the amount of mayonnaise and sour cream to achieve your desired creaminess. Season with salt and pepper to taste.
4. **Combine and Chill:**
   - Pour the dressing over the salad ingredients in the bowl. Gently toss until everything is well coated with the dressing.
5. **Chill and Serve:**
   - Cover the salad with plastic wrap and refrigerate for at least 1 hour before serving to allow the flavors to meld.
   - Garnish with chopped fresh dill before serving.

Tips for Making Olivier Salad:

- **Variations:** Olivier Salad is very versatile. You can add or omit ingredients based on your preferences. Some variations include adding diced boiled beets, pickled herring, or even capers for extra flavor.
- **Make Ahead:** Olivier Salad can be made a day in advance and stored in the refrigerator. It actually tastes better after the flavors have had time to blend together.
- **Dressing Adjustments:** Adjust the amount of mayonnaise and sour cream based on how creamy you like your salad. Some prefer a tangier dressing, in which case you can add more Dijon mustard or a splash of vinegar.
- **Serve:** Olivier Salad is typically served as a side dish or appetizer at celebrations, holidays, and gatherings. It pairs well with grilled meats, sandwiches, or can be enjoyed on its own.

Olivier Salad is a classic Russian dish that has stood the test of time, loved for its hearty ingredients and creamy dressing. It's a comforting and satisfying salad that's perfect for any occasion.

Mimosa Salad (Layered Salad with Fish)

Ingredients:

- 3 medium potatoes, boiled and grated
- 3 medium carrots, boiled and grated
- 1 can (7 oz) canned tuna or salmon, drained and flaked
- 4 hard-boiled eggs, separated (yolks and whites separated and grated separately)
- 1 small onion, finely chopped
- 1/2 cup mayonnaise (plus more for garnish)
- Salt and pepper, to taste
- Fresh dill, chopped, for garnish (optional)

Instructions:

1. **Prepare the Ingredients:**
    - Boil the potatoes and carrots until tender. Cool, peel, and grate them using a coarse grater.
    - Boil the eggs until hard-boiled. Separate the yolks from the whites. Grate the yolks and whites separately using a fine grater or sieve.
2. **Assemble the Salad:**
    - In a large serving bowl or on a platter, create the first layer with half of the grated potatoes. Press down gently to form an even layer.
    - Spread half of the mayonnaise evenly over the potato layer.
    - Next, spread the finely chopped onion evenly over the mayonnaise layer.
    - Create the next layer with all of the flaked tuna or salmon, spreading it evenly.
    - Top the fish layer with the grated carrots, pressing down gently.
    - Spread the remaining mayonnaise evenly over the carrot layer.

- Finally, spread the remaining grated potatoes over the mayonnaise layer, forming the top layer of the salad.
3. **Finish and Garnish:**
    - Sprinkle the grated egg whites evenly over the top layer of potatoes.
    - Next, evenly sprinkle the grated egg yolks over the egg whites to create a yellow mimosa flower-like appearance.
    - Garnish with fresh chopped dill if desired.
4. **Chill and Serve:**
    - Cover the salad with plastic wrap and refrigerate for at least 1 hour before serving to allow the flavors to meld together.

Tips for Making Mimosa Salad:

- **Fish Variation:** Mimosa Salad traditionally uses canned tuna or salmon, but you can also use other types of canned fish like sardines or mackerel.
- **Vegetables:** The potatoes and carrots should be finely grated to ensure even layers and a smooth texture.
- **Presentation:** Use a round serving dish or mold to create a neat and uniform shape for the salad when serving.
- **Make Ahead:** Mimosa Salad can be made a day in advance and stored covered in the refrigerator. This allows the flavors to develop even more.
- **Serve:** Mimosa Salad is typically served as an appetizer or side dish at celebrations, holidays, and gatherings. It pairs well with bread, crackers, or as part of a larger spread of Russian salads.

Mimosa Salad is a classic dish in Russian cuisine known for its colorful layers and delicate flavors. It's a beautiful and delicious addition to any table, especially for festive occasions.

Herring Under a Fur Coat (Layered Herring Salad)

Ingredients:

- 2-3 salted herring fillets, boneless and skinless
- 3 medium potatoes, boiled and grated
- 3 medium carrots, boiled and grated
- 2-3 medium beets, boiled and grated
- 1 large onion, finely chopped
- 2-3 hard-boiled eggs, separated (yolks and whites grated separately)
- 1 cup mayonnaise (plus more for garnish)
- Salt and pepper, to taste
- Fresh dill, chopped, for garnish (optional)

Instructions:

1. **Prepare the Ingredients:**

- Boil the potatoes, carrots, and beets until tender. Cool, peel, and grate them using a coarse grater.
- Boil the eggs until hard-boiled. Separate the yolks from the whites. Grate the yolks and whites separately using a fine grater or sieve.

2. **Prepare the Herring:**
    - If using salted herring fillets, rinse them under cold water to remove excess salt. Pat dry with paper towels and dice into small pieces.
3. **Assemble the Salad:**
    - In a large serving dish or on a platter, create the first layer with half of the grated potatoes. Press down gently to form an even layer.
    - Spread a thin layer of mayonnaise evenly over the potato layer.
    - Create the next layer with all of the diced herring, spreading it evenly over the mayonnaise layer.
    - Spread another layer of mayonnaise evenly over the herring layer.
    - Create the next layer with all of the grated carrots, pressing down gently.
    - Spread another layer of mayonnaise evenly over the carrot layer.
    - Create the next layer with all of the grated beets, pressing down gently.
    - Spread another layer of mayonnaise evenly over the beet layer.
    - Sprinkle the finely chopped onion evenly over the mayonnaise layer.
    - Finally, spread the remaining grated potatoes evenly over the onion layer, forming the top layer of the salad.
4. **Finish and Garnish:**
    - Sprinkle the grated egg whites evenly over the top layer of potatoes.
    - Next, evenly sprinkle the grated egg yolks over the egg whites to create a colorful and decorative appearance.
    - Garnish with fresh chopped dill if desired.
5. **Chill and Serve:**
    - Cover the salad with plastic wrap and refrigerate for at least 2-3 hours before serving to allow the flavors to meld together.

Tips for Making Herring Under a Fur Coat:

- **Herring:** You can use either salted herring fillets or marinated herring for this salad. If using salted herring, make sure to rinse it well to remove excess salt.
- **Mayonnaise:** Use good quality mayonnaise for the best flavor. Some recipes also incorporate sour cream for a tangier dressing.
- **Presentation:** Use a deep serving dish or mold to create a neat and uniform shape for the salad when serving.
- **Make Ahead:** Herring Under a Fur Coat can be made a day in advance and stored covered in the refrigerator. This allows the flavors to develop even more.
- **Serve:** Herring Under a Fur Coat is typically served as a festive appetizer or side dish at celebrations, holidays, and gatherings. It pairs well with rye bread or as part of a larger spread of Russian salads.

Herring Under a Fur Coat is a classic dish in Russian cuisine known for its beautiful layers and rich flavors. It's a perfect addition to any festive table and is sure to impress with its vibrant colors and delicious combination of ingredients.

Selyodka Pod Shuboy (Herring Under a Fur Coat)

Ingredients:

- 2-3 salted herring fillets, boneless and skinless
- 3 medium potatoes, boiled and grated
- 3 medium carrots, boiled and grated
- 2-3 medium beets, boiled and grated
- 1 large onion, finely chopped
- 2-3 hard-boiled eggs, separated (yolks and whites grated separately)
- 1 cup mayonnaise (plus more for garnish)
- Salt and pepper, to taste
- Fresh dill, chopped, for garnish (optional)

Instructions:

1. **Prepare the Ingredients:**
   - Boil the potatoes, carrots, and beets until tender. Cool, peel, and grate them using a coarse grater.
   - Boil the eggs until hard-boiled. Separate the yolks from the whites. Grate the yolks and whites separately using a fine grater or sieve.
2. **Prepare the Herring:**
   - Rinse the salted herring fillets under cold water to remove excess salt. Pat dry with paper towels and dice into small pieces.
3. **Assemble the Salad:**
   - In a large serving dish or on a platter, create the first layer with half of the grated potatoes. Press down gently to form an even layer.
   - Spread a thin layer of mayonnaise evenly over the potato layer.
   - Create the next layer with all of the diced herring, spreading it evenly over the mayonnaise layer.
   - Spread another layer of mayonnaise evenly over the herring layer.
   - Create the next layer with all of the grated carrots, pressing down gently.
   - Spread another layer of mayonnaise evenly over the carrot layer.
   - Create the next layer with all of the grated beets, pressing down gently.
   - Spread another layer of mayonnaise evenly over the beet layer.
   - Sprinkle the finely chopped onion evenly over the mayonnaise layer.
   - Finally, spread the remaining grated potatoes evenly over the onion layer, forming the top layer of the salad.
4. **Finish and Garnish:**
   - Sprinkle the grated egg whites evenly over the top layer of potatoes.

- Next, evenly sprinkle the grated egg yolks over the egg whites to create a colorful and decorative appearance.
- Garnish with fresh chopped dill if desired.
5. **Chill and Serve:**
    - Cover the salad with plastic wrap and refrigerate for at least 2-3 hours before serving to allow the flavors to meld together.

Tips for Making Selyodka Pod Shuboy:

- **Herring:** Ensure that the herring is well-rinsed to remove excess salt if using salted herring fillets.
- **Mayonnaise:** Use a good quality mayonnaise for the best flavor. Some recipes also incorporate sour cream for a tangier dressing.
- **Presentation:** Use a deep serving dish or mold to create a neat and uniform shape for the salad when serving.
- **Make Ahead:** Selyodka Pod Shuboy can be made a day in advance and stored covered in the refrigerator. This allows the flavors to develop even more.
- **Serve:** This salad is typically served as a festive appetizer or side dish at celebrations, holidays, and gatherings. It pairs well with rye bread or as part of a larger spread of Russian salads.

Selyodka Pod Shuboy is a classic dish in Russian cuisine known for its beautiful layers and rich flavors. It's a perfect addition to any festive table and is sure to impress with its vibrant colors and delicious combination of ingredients.

Zakuski (Russian Appetizers)

Traditional Zakuski Ideas:

1. **Pickled Vegetables (Marinated Vegetables):**
    - Pickled cucumbers (огурцы маринованные)
    - Pickled tomatoes (помидоры маринованные)
    - Pickled mushrooms (грибы маринованные)
2. **Salted Herring (Сельдь соленая):**
    - Served with onions, bread, or boiled potatoes.
3. **Caviar (Икра):**
    - Red caviar (красная икра) or black caviar (черная икра) served on blini or bread.
4. **Smoked Fish:**
    - Smoked salmon (лосось копченый) or smoked trout (форель копченая), served with horseradish or mustard sauce.
5. **Meat and Sausage Platters:**
    - Assorted cold cuts (колбаса), such as salami, ham, and smoked sausages.
6. **Piroshki (Пирожки):**
    - Small baked or fried buns filled with meat, mushrooms, cabbage, or potatoes.

7. **Salads:**
    - Olivier Salad (салат Оливье), also known as Russian Salad, made with potatoes, carrots, peas, pickles, eggs, and mayonnaise.
    - Vinegret (винегрет), a beetroot salad with potatoes, carrots, pickles, onions, and a light dressing.
8. **Cheese Platters:**
    - Assorted cheeses (сыр), such as Russian varieties like Adygea cheese, served with crackers or bread.
9. **Canapés and Open-faced Sandwiches:**
    - Topped with various spreads like butter, caviar, fish, or vegetables.
10. **Vodka and Accompaniments:**
    - Chilled vodka (водка) served with zakuski to enhance the flavors and experience.

Serving Tips:

- **Presentation:** Arrange zakuski attractively on a platter or individual plates.
- **Accompaniments:** Serve with rye bread, blini (thin pancakes), or breadsticks.
- **Variety:** Offer a variety of textures and flavors to appeal to different tastes.
- **Timing:** Serve zakuski before the main course to stimulate the appetite and complement drinks like vodka or wine.

Zakuski are an integral part of Russian cuisine, often enjoyed during celebrations, holidays, or gatherings with friends and family. They showcase a range of flavors and ingredients that reflect the rich culinary traditions of Russia.

Khachapuri (Georgian Cheese Bread)

Ingredients:

For the Dough:

- 2 cups all-purpose flour
- 1 teaspoon instant yeast
- 1 teaspoon sugar
- 1 teaspoon salt
- 1/2 cup lukewarm water
- 1/2 cup lukewarm milk
- 2 tablespoons olive oil

For the Filling:

- 2 cups grated sulguni cheese (or a mixture of mozzarella and feta cheese)
- 1/2 cup grated mozzarella cheese (for additional stretchiness)
- 1 egg, plus extra for topping

- 2 tablespoons butter, melted (for brushing)

Instructions:

1. **Prepare the Dough:**
   - In a large mixing bowl, combine the flour, instant yeast, sugar, and salt.
   - Make a well in the center and pour in the lukewarm water, lukewarm milk, and olive oil.
   - Stir until the dough comes together. Knead the dough on a floured surface for about 5-7 minutes until smooth and elastic.
   - Place the dough in a greased bowl, cover with a kitchen towel, and let it rise in a warm place for about 1 hour or until doubled in size.
2. **Prepare the Filling:**
   - In a bowl, combine the grated sulguni cheese (or mozzarella and feta), grated mozzarella cheese, and 1 egg. Mix well until evenly combined.
3. **Assemble the Khachapuri:**
   - Preheat your oven to 475°F (245°C). Place a pizza stone or baking sheet in the oven to preheat.
   - Punch down the risen dough and divide it into 2 equal portions.
   - On a floured surface, roll out each portion of dough into an oval or boat shape, about 1/4 inch thick.
   - Transfer each dough oval to a parchment-lined baking sheet or a pizza peel (if using a pizza stone).
   - Spoon half of the cheese mixture onto each dough oval, leaving a border around the edges.
   - Fold the edges of the dough over the cheese, pinching the ends to form a boat shape. Leave the center open to form a well for the egg.
4. **Bake the Khachapuri:**
   - Crack an egg into the center well of each khachapuri.
   - Brush the edges of the dough with melted butter.
   - Carefully transfer the khachapuri to the preheated baking stone or baking sheet in the oven.
   - Bake for 12-15 minutes or until the crust is golden brown and the cheese is melted and bubbly.
5. **Serve:**
   - Remove from the oven and immediately brush the edges with more melted butter.
   - Serve hot, allowing each person to mix the egg into the hot cheese filling before eating.

Tips for Making Khachapuri:

- **Cheese:** Traditional khachapuri uses sulguni cheese, which is a Georgian cheese. If unavailable, you can use a combination of mozzarella and feta cheese for a similar flavor.
- **Shape:** While Adjarian khachapuri is shaped like a boat with an egg on top, there are other shapes like Imeretian khachapuri (round with cheese filling) and Megrelian khachapuri (similar to Imeretian but with extra cheese and butter on top).
- **Egg:** The egg can be cracked directly into the cheese filling before baking or added halfway through baking, depending on preference for the yolk's doneness.

Khachapuri is a delicious and comforting dish that's enjoyed throughout Georgia and beyond, often served as a main course or even as a snack. It's perfect for sharing with family and friends, especially when freshly baked and hot out of the oven.

Chakhokhbili (Georgian Chicken Stew)

Ingredients:

- 1 whole chicken (about 3-4 lbs), cut into pieces
- 2 tablespoons vegetable oil
- 2 onions, finely chopped
- 4 garlic cloves, minced
- 3 large tomatoes, peeled and chopped (or 1 can of diced tomatoes)
- 1 green bell pepper, chopped
- 1 red bell pepper, chopped
- 1 teaspoon paprika
- 1/2 teaspoon ground coriander
- 1/2 teaspoon ground fenugreek (optional)
- 1/2 teaspoon dried marigold (optional)
- Salt and pepper, to taste
- Fresh cilantro or parsley, chopped, for garnish

Instructions:

1. **Prepare the Chicken:**
    - Rinse the chicken pieces under cold water and pat them dry with paper towels. Cut the chicken into serving pieces, such as legs, thighs, wings, and breasts.
2. **Sauté the Onions and Garlic:**
    - Heat the vegetable oil in a large, heavy-bottomed pot or Dutch oven over medium heat.
    - Add the finely chopped onions and sauté for about 5 minutes until they start to soften and become translucent.
    - Add the minced garlic and sauté for another 1-2 minutes until fragrant.
3. **Cook the Chicken:**
    - Increase the heat to medium-high. Add the chicken pieces to the pot, skin-side down, and cook for about 5-7 minutes until they are lightly browned.

- Turn the chicken pieces over and cook for another 5 minutes.
4. **Add Tomatoes and Peppers:**
    - Add the chopped tomatoes, green bell pepper, and red bell pepper to the pot. Stir well to combine.
5. **Season and Simmer:**
    - Add the paprika, ground coriander, ground fenugreek (if using), dried marigold (if using), salt, and pepper to taste. Stir to combine all the ingredients.
    - Bring the mixture to a boil, then reduce the heat to low. Cover the pot with a lid and simmer for about 30-40 minutes, stirring occasionally, until the chicken is cooked through and tender.
6. **Finish and Serve:**
    - Once the chicken is cooked, taste and adjust the seasoning if needed.
    - Remove the pot from the heat and sprinkle chopped fresh cilantro or parsley over the Chakhokhbili.
    - Serve hot, traditionally with bread or over rice or mashed potatoes.

Tips for Making Chakhokhbili:

- **Chicken:** You can use a whole chicken cut into pieces or chicken thighs and drumsticks for this recipe. Make sure to brown the chicken pieces well for added flavor.
- **Tomatoes:** Fresh tomatoes are traditional, but you can also use canned diced tomatoes for convenience. If using fresh tomatoes, blanch them in hot water for a minute, peel, and then chop.
- **Spices:** Ground coriander and paprika are essential spices in Chakhokhbili. Fenugreek and marigold add a unique Georgian flavor profile, but they are optional and can be omitted if unavailable.
- **Variations:** Some recipes include additional herbs like basil or tarragon for extra flavor. Adjust the seasonings and spices according to your taste preferences.

Chakhokhbili is a comforting and aromatic dish that showcases the vibrant flavors of Georgian cuisine. It's perfect for family meals or gatherings, offering a delicious blend of chicken, tomatoes, and peppers with a hint of aromatic spices.

Khinkali (Georgian Dumplings)

Ingredients:

For the Dough:

- 2 cups all-purpose flour, plus extra for dusting
- 1/2 teaspoon salt
- 1/2 cup lukewarm water

For the Filling:

- 1 lb ground beef or pork (or a mixture of both)
- 1 medium onion, finely chopped
- 2-3 garlic cloves, minced
- 1 tablespoon fresh cilantro, finely chopped
- 1 tablespoon fresh parsley, finely chopped
- 1/2 teaspoon ground coriander
- 1/2 teaspoon ground cumin
- 1/2 teaspoon ground black pepper
- Salt, to taste

Instructions:

1. **Prepare the Dough:**
   - In a large mixing bowl, combine the flour and salt.
   - Gradually add the lukewarm water, stirring with a spoon or your hands until the dough comes together.
   - Knead the dough on a lightly floured surface for about 8-10 minutes until smooth and elastic.
   - Cover the dough with a damp kitchen towel and let it rest for at least 30 minutes.
2. **Prepare the Filling:**
   - In a separate bowl, combine the ground meat, finely chopped onion, minced garlic, chopped cilantro, chopped parsley, ground coriander, ground cumin, ground black pepper, and salt to taste.
   - Mix well until all the ingredients are evenly incorporated. The filling should be well-seasoned and moist.
3. **Form the Dumplings (Khinkali):**
   - Divide the rested dough into small balls, about the size of a walnut.
   - On a lightly floured surface, roll out each ball of dough into a thin circle, about 3-4 inches in diameter.
   - Place a spoonful of the meat filling (about 1-2 tablespoons) in the center of each dough circle.
4. **Shape the Khinkali:**
   - To shape the khinkali, gather the edges of the dough circle together over the filling to create pleats or folds. Pinch and twist the top to seal the dumpling, leaving a small opening at the top.
   - The traditional shape is like a small purse with a twisted top, resembling a small bag or hat.
5. **Cook the Khinkali:**
   - Bring a large pot of salted water to a boil.
   - Carefully place the khinkali in the boiling water, making sure they don't stick to the bottom of the pot. Cook in batches if necessary.
   - Boil the khinkali for about 8-10 minutes, or until they float to the surface and the meat is cooked through.
6. **Serve the Khinkali:**

- Remove the cooked khinkali from the water using a slotted spoon and transfer them to a serving platter or individual plates.
- Serve hot, traditionally with a side of black pepper and a sprinkle of ground sumac or vinegar on the top.

Tips for Making Khinkali:

- **Filling Variations:** Besides beef or pork, you can use lamb, chicken, or a mixture of meats. Adjust the seasoning according to the type of meat used.
- **Twisted Top:** The twisted top of the khinkali serves as a convenient handle for eating. It's traditional to hold the khinkali by the twisted top and take a small bite to release the steam before eating the filling.
- **Boiling Time:** Ensure the khinkali are fully cooked through by boiling them until they float to the surface. Avoid overcrowding the pot to prevent them from sticking together.
- **Serving Suggestions:** Khinkali are often served with a sprinkle of ground black pepper and a side of Georgian tkemali sauce (plum sauce) or a simple vinegar and garlic dipping sauce.

Khinkali are not only delicious but also a fun dish to make with friends and family, especially when shaping and sealing the dumplings. They represent the rich culinary heritage of Georgia and are enjoyed for their juicy, flavorful filling and unique shape.

Lobio (Georgian Bean Stew)

Ingredients:

- 2 cups dried red kidney beans (or 4 cups canned red kidney beans, drained and rinsed)
- 1 large onion, finely chopped
- 3-4 cloves garlic, minced
- 2 tablespoons vegetable oil
- 2 tablespoons tomato paste
- 1 large tomato, diced (or 1/2 cup canned diced tomatoes)
- 1 teaspoon ground coriander
- 1 teaspoon ground fenugreek (optional)
- 1/2 teaspoon ground marigold (optional)
- 1/2 teaspoon ground hot red pepper (optional, adjust to taste)
- 1 bay leaf
- Salt and pepper, to taste
- Fresh parsley or cilantro, chopped, for garnish

Instructions:

1. **Prepare the Beans:**
   - If using dried kidney beans, rinse them under cold water and soak them in water overnight. Drain and rinse the soaked beans before cooking.

- Place the soaked or canned beans in a large pot and cover with water. Bring to a boil, then reduce the heat to low and simmer until the beans are tender, about 1-1.5 hours for dried beans. Drain and set aside.

2. **Cook the Aromatics:**
   - In a large, heavy-bottomed pot or Dutch oven, heat the vegetable oil over medium heat.
   - Add the finely chopped onion and sauté for 5-7 minutes until softened and translucent.
   - Add the minced garlic and sauté for another 1-2 minutes until fragrant.
3. **Add Tomato Paste and Spices:**
   - Stir in the tomato paste and cook for 1-2 minutes to deepen the flavor.
   - Add the diced tomato (or canned diced tomatoes), ground coriander, ground fenugreek (if using), ground marigold (if using), ground hot red pepper (if using), and bay leaf. Stir well to combine.
4. **Simmer the Stew:**
   - Add the cooked kidney beans to the pot with the aromatics and spices.
   - Season with salt and pepper to taste. Stir well to combine all the ingredients.
   - Bring the mixture to a simmer over low heat. Cover the pot with a lid and cook for 20-30 minutes, stirring occasionally, to allow the flavors to meld together.
5. **Serve the Lobio:**
   - Remove the bay leaf from the pot.
   - Serve the lobio hot, garnished with freshly chopped parsley or cilantro.
   - Lobio is traditionally served with Georgian bread (such as shotis puri) or cornbread (mchadi).

Tips for Making Lobio:

- **Variations:** You can customize lobio by adding other vegetables such as bell peppers or carrots. Some recipes also include ground walnuts for added texture and richness.
- **Spices:** Adjust the amount of ground hot red pepper according to your taste preference. Georgian cuisine often uses a blend of spices that contribute to its unique flavor profile.
- **Storage:** Leftover lobio can be stored in an airtight container in the refrigerator for up to 3-4 days. Reheat gently on the stove or in the microwave before serving.
- **Garnish:** Fresh herbs like parsley or cilantro not only add color but also enhance the freshness of the dish.

Lobio is a comforting and nutritious dish that highlights the use of beans and aromatic spices in Georgian cuisine. It's perfect for vegetarians and meat-eaters alike, offering a satisfying meal that pairs well with Georgian bread and a side of fresh vegetables.

Adjaruli Khachapuri (Georgian Cheese Bread with Egg)

Ingredients:

For the Dough:

- 2 cups all-purpose flour
- 1 teaspoon active dry yeast
- 1 teaspoon sugar
- 1/2 teaspoon salt
- 3/4 cup lukewarm water
- 1 tablespoon vegetable oil

For the Filling:

- 1 cup grated mozzarella cheese
- 1 cup grated feta cheese
- 1/2 cup grated sulguni cheese (or substitute with more mozzarella or feta)
- 1 egg, lightly beaten
- 1 tablespoon unsalted butter, diced into small pieces

For the Topping:

- 1 egg
- 1 tablespoon unsalted butter

Instructions:

1. **Prepare the Dough:**
    - In a small bowl, combine the lukewarm water, sugar, and yeast. Let it sit for 5-10 minutes until foamy.
    - In a large mixing bowl, combine the flour and salt. Make a well in the center and pour in the yeast mixture and vegetable oil.
    - Mix until a dough forms. Knead the dough on a lightly floured surface for about 8-10 minutes until smooth and elastic.
    - Place the dough in a lightly oiled bowl, cover with a damp cloth, and let it rise in a warm place for 1-1.5 hours or until doubled in size.
2. **Prepare the Filling:**
    - In a bowl, combine the grated mozzarella, feta, and sulguni cheeses. Mix well.
3. **Shape and Assemble the Khachapuri:**
    - Preheat your oven to 475°F (245°C) and place a baking stone or baking sheet in the oven to heat up.
    - Punch down the risen dough and divide it into two equal portions.
    - Roll out each portion into an oval or boat shape, about 10-12 inches long and 5-6 inches wide.
    - Transfer the rolled-out dough to a parchment-lined baking sheet or a well-floured pizza peel if using a baking stone.
4. **Add the Cheese Filling:**
    - Divide the cheese mixture evenly between the two pieces of dough, spreading it out in the center, leaving about 1 inch around the edges.
5. **Shape the Boat:**

- Fold the edges of the dough towards the center, pinching them together to form a boat shape with raised edges to hold the cheese filling.
6. **Add Egg and Butter:**
    - Crack one egg into the center of each khachapuri boat.
    - Dot the diced butter pieces around the cheese and egg in each boat.
7. **Bake the Khachapuri:**
    - Carefully slide the khachapuri onto the preheated baking stone or baking sheet in the oven.
    - Bake for about 12-15 minutes, or until the crust is golden brown and the cheese is bubbly and melted.
8. **Finish and Serve:**
    - Remove from the oven and immediately place a tablespoon of butter in the center of each khachapuri boat.
    - Use a spoon to mix the butter with the hot egg and cheese, creating a creamy texture.
    - Serve hot, traditionally with extra butter on the side for dipping.

Tips for Making Adjaruli Khachapuri:

- **Cheese:** Use a combination of cheeses for the filling to achieve the traditional flavor. Sulguni cheese can be difficult to find outside of Georgia, so mozzarella and feta are good substitutes.
- **Egg:** The egg should be added raw before baking. It will cook in the oven as the khachapuri bakes, creating a creamy texture with the melted cheese and butter.
- **Butter:** Butter is an essential part of finishing Adjaruli Khachapuri. It adds richness and enhances the flavors of the cheese and egg mixture.
- **Serve Immediately:** Adjaruli Khachapuri is best enjoyed hot and fresh from the oven. The combination of melted cheese, egg, and butter is comforting and satisfying.

Adjaruli Khachapuri is a beloved Georgian dish that showcases the rich culinary traditions of the region. It's perfect for a special brunch or as a hearty meal any time of day.

Kubdari (Georgian Meat Pie)

Ingredients:

For the Dough:

- 4 cups all-purpose flour
- 1 teaspoon active dry yeast
- 1 teaspoon sugar
- 1 cup lukewarm water
- 1/4 cup olive oil
- 1 teaspoon salt

For the Filling:

- 1 lb (450g) ground beef or pork (or a mixture of both)
- 1 large onion, finely chopped
- 2 cloves garlic, minced
- 1 tablespoon tomato paste
- 1 teaspoon ground coriander
- 1 teaspoon ground fenugreek (optional)
- 1/2 teaspoon ground hot red pepper (adjust to taste)
- Salt and pepper, to taste
- Fresh parsley, chopped, for garnish

Instructions:

1. **Prepare the Dough:**
    - In a small bowl, combine the lukewarm water, sugar, and yeast. Let it sit for 5-10 minutes until foamy.
    - In a large mixing bowl, combine the flour and salt. Make a well in the center and pour in the yeast mixture and olive oil.
    - Mix until a dough forms. Knead the dough on a lightly floured surface for about 8-10 minutes until smooth and elastic.
    - Place the dough in a lightly oiled bowl, cover with a damp cloth, and let it rise in a warm place for 1-1.5 hours or until doubled in size.
2. **Prepare the Filling:**
    - In a large skillet, heat a tablespoon of olive oil over medium heat.
    - Add the finely chopped onion and sauté for 5-7 minutes until softened and translucent.
    - Add the minced garlic and sauté for another 1-2 minutes until fragrant.
    - Add the ground beef or pork to the skillet and cook until browned, breaking it up with a spoon as it cooks.
    - Stir in the tomato paste, ground coriander, ground fenugreek (if using), ground hot red pepper (if using), salt, and pepper. Cook for another 2-3 minutes, stirring occasionally. Remove from heat and let the filling cool slightly.
3. **Assemble the Kubdari:**
    - Preheat your oven to 400°F (200°C). Line a baking sheet with parchment paper.
    - Divide the risen dough into 6 equal portions. Roll out each portion into a circle about 8-10 inches in diameter and 1/4 inch thick.
    - Place a generous amount of the meat filling (about 1/2 cup) onto one half of each dough circle, leaving a border around the edges.
    - Fold the other half of the dough over the filling to create a semi-circle shape. Press the edges firmly to seal.
    - Transfer the filled kubdari to the prepared baking sheet.
4. **Bake the Kubdari:**
    - Brush the tops of the kubdari with olive oil.

- Bake in the preheated oven for 20-25 minutes, or until the crust is golden brown and cooked through.
5. **Serve the Kubdari:**
    - Remove from the oven and let the kubdari cool slightly before serving.
    - Garnish with chopped fresh parsley before serving.

Tips for Making Kubdari:

- **Meat Filling:** You can use either ground beef, pork, or a combination of both for the filling. Ensure the meat is well-seasoned with spices and cooked thoroughly before filling the dough.
- **Spices:** Georgian cuisine often uses a blend of aromatic spices such as coriander, fenugreek, and hot red pepper. Adjust the amount of hot pepper according to your preference for spiciness.
- **Storage:** Kubdari can be stored in an airtight container in the refrigerator for up to 3 days. Reheat gently in the oven or microwave before serving.
- **Serve with:** Kubdari is traditionally enjoyed on its own or with a side of fresh vegetables, pickles, or Georgian sauces like tkemali.

Kubdari is a delightful Georgian meat pie that combines flavorful meat filling with a soft, slightly crispy dough. It's perfect for a satisfying meal and showcases the rich culinary heritage of Georgia.

Mtsvadi (Georgian Shish Kebabs)

Ingredients:

For the Marinade:

- 1 lb (450g) beef or pork, cut into 1-inch cubes
- 1 large onion, finely chopped
- 3 cloves garlic, minced
- 1/4 cup white wine vinegar or red wine vinegar
- 1/4 cup olive oil
- 1/4 cup water
- 1 teaspoon ground coriander
- 1 teaspoon ground fenugreek (optional)
- 1/2 teaspoon ground hot red pepper (adjust to taste)
- Salt and pepper, to taste

For Serving:

- Freshly chopped parsley or cilantro
- Sliced onions (optional)
- Sliced tomatoes (optional)

- Pita bread or lavash (optional)

Instructions:

1. **Prepare the Marinade:**
   - In a large bowl, combine the finely chopped onion, minced garlic, vinegar, olive oil, water, ground coriander, ground fenugreek (if using), ground hot red pepper (adjust to taste), salt, and pepper. Mix well.
   - Add the cubed meat to the marinade, ensuring all pieces are well coated. Cover the bowl with plastic wrap or transfer to a resealable plastic bag. Marinate in the refrigerator for at least 2 hours, preferably overnight, to allow the flavors to develop.
2. **Prepare the Skewers:**
   - If using wooden skewers, soak them in water for at least 30 minutes to prevent burning during grilling.
   - Thread the marinated meat onto the skewers, evenly distributing the pieces and leaving a bit of space between each piece for even cooking.
3. **Grill the Mtsvadi:**
   - Preheat your grill to medium-high heat.
   - Place the skewers on the grill and cook for about 10-15 minutes, turning occasionally, until the meat is cooked to your desired doneness and has nice grill marks.
   - While grilling, baste the skewers with any remaining marinade to keep them moist and flavorful.
4. **Serve the Mtsvadi:**
   - Once cooked, remove the skewers from the grill and let them rest for a few minutes.
   - Serve the Mtsvadi hot, garnished with freshly chopped parsley or cilantro.
   - Optionally, serve with sliced onions, tomatoes, and pita bread or lavash on the side.

Tips for Making Mtsvadi:

- **Meat:** You can use beef, pork, or a combination of both for Mtsvadi. Choose cuts that are suitable for grilling and cut them into uniform pieces for even cooking.
- **Marinating Time:** Marinating the meat for at least 2 hours allows the flavors to penetrate the meat thoroughly. Overnight marinating will yield even better results.
- **Grilling:** Ensure your grill is hot before placing the skewers on it. This helps to sear the meat and lock in the juices.
- **Serving Suggestions:** Mtsvadi is traditionally served with fresh herbs, sliced onions, and tomatoes. It can also be enjoyed with Georgian bread (shotis puri) or as part of a larger Georgian feast.

Mtsvadi is a delicious and flavorful dish that showcases the simplicity and richness of Georgian cuisine. It's perfect for grilling outdoors and is sure to be a hit at any barbecue or gathering.

Pkhali (Georgian Vegetable Pâté)

Ingredients:

For the Walnut Paste:

- 1 cup walnuts, shelled
- 2 cloves garlic, minced
- 1 tablespoon white wine vinegar or red wine vinegar
- 1 tablespoon ground coriander
- 1/2 teaspoon ground fenugreek (optional)
- 1/2 teaspoon ground hot red pepper (adjust to taste)
- Salt, to taste
- Pepper, to taste
- Water, as needed

For the Vegetable Base:

- 1 lb (450g) spinach leaves (fresh or frozen)
- 1 bunch of cilantro, chopped
- 1 bunch of parsley, chopped
- 1 medium onion, finely chopped
- 2-3 green onions, finely chopped (optional)
- 2 tablespoons vegetable oil
- Salt, to taste
- Pepper, to taste

For Garnish:

- Pomegranate seeds (optional)
- Chopped fresh herbs (cilantro, parsley)

Instructions:

1. **Prepare the Walnut Paste:**
    - In a food processor or blender, combine the walnuts, minced garlic, vinegar, ground coriander, ground fenugreek (if using), ground hot red pepper (adjust to taste), salt, and pepper.
    - Pulse until the mixture forms a coarse paste. Add a little water, a tablespoon at a time, if needed to help blend into a smooth consistency. The paste should be thick but spreadable. Set aside.
2. **Prepare the Vegetable Base:**

- If using fresh spinach, wash thoroughly. If using frozen spinach, thaw and drain excess water.
- In a large pot, heat the vegetable oil over medium heat. Add the finely chopped onion and sauté until translucent, about 5-7 minutes.
- Add the spinach to the pot and cook until wilted, stirring occasionally. If using fresh spinach, it will cook down quickly. If using frozen spinach, cook until heated through.
- Remove from heat and let the spinach mixture cool slightly.
3. **Combine Walnut Paste and Vegetable Base:**
    - In a large mixing bowl, combine the walnut paste with the cooked spinach mixture, chopped cilantro, chopped parsley, and green onions (if using).
    - Mix well until all ingredients are evenly distributed. Taste and adjust seasoning with salt and pepper as needed.
4. **Shape and Serve Pkhali:**
    - Transfer the mixture to a serving dish or individual small bowls.
    - Using a spoon or spatula, smooth the top of the Pkhali mixture to create an even surface.
    - Optionally, garnish with pomegranate seeds and chopped fresh herbs (cilantro, parsley) for color and additional flavor.
5. **Chill and Serve:**
    - Cover the Pkhali dish with plastic wrap and refrigerate for at least 1-2 hours before serving. Chilling helps the flavors meld together.
6. **Serve Cold:**
    - Serve Pkhali cold as a delicious appetizer or side dish. It can be enjoyed on its own or with bread, such as Georgian shotis puri or lavash.

Tips for Making Pkhali:

- **Variations:** Pkhali can be made with various vegetables such as beet greens, cabbage, or carrots. Adjust the cooking time and preparation method accordingly for different vegetables.
- **Consistency:** The texture of Pkhali should be firm enough to hold its shape when served but still spreadable. Add more walnut paste if a thicker consistency is desired.
- **Storage:** Leftover Pkhali can be stored in an airtight container in the refrigerator for up to 3 days. Allow it to come to room temperature before serving leftovers.

Pkhali is a nutritious and flavorful dish that showcases the fresh herbs and spices characteristic of Georgian cuisine. It's perfect for gatherings and pairs wonderfully with other Georgian dishes or as part of a mezze platter.

Ajapsandali (Georgian Vegetable Stew)

Ingredients:

- 2 medium eggplants, diced into 1-inch cubes

- 2 medium tomatoes, diced
- 1 large onion, finely chopped
- 2-3 cloves garlic, minced
- 1 red bell pepper, diced
- 1 green bell pepper, diced
- 1 tablespoon tomato paste
- 1 teaspoon ground coriander
- 1/2 teaspoon ground fenugreek (optional)
- 1/2 teaspoon ground hot red pepper (adjust to taste)
- Salt, to taste
- Pepper, to taste
- Fresh parsley or cilantro, chopped, for garnish
- Olive oil, for cooking

Instructions:

1. **Prepare the Eggplants:**
    - Dice the eggplants into 1-inch cubes. Place them in a colander, sprinkle with salt, and let them sit for about 20-30 minutes. This helps draw out any bitterness from the eggplants. Rinse thoroughly and pat dry with paper towels.
2. **Sauté the Vegetables:**
    - In a large skillet or Dutch oven, heat a few tablespoons of olive oil over medium heat.
    - Add the chopped onion and sauté until translucent, about 5-7 minutes.
    - Add the minced garlic and sauté for another 1-2 minutes until fragrant.
3. **Cook the Bell Peppers:**
    - Add the diced bell peppers (both red and green) to the skillet. Sauté for 5-7 minutes until they start to soften.
4. **Add Tomatoes and Tomato Paste:**
    - Stir in the diced tomatoes and tomato paste. Cook for another 5 minutes, stirring occasionally, until the tomatoes begin to break down and release their juices.
5. **Season the Stew:**
    - Add the diced eggplants to the skillet. Season with ground coriander, ground fenugreek (if using), ground hot red pepper (adjust to taste), salt, and pepper. Mix well to combine all the ingredients.
6. **Simmer the Stew:**
    - Reduce the heat to low, cover the skillet, and let the stew simmer gently for about 20-25 minutes, or until the vegetables are tender and cooked through. Stir occasionally to prevent sticking and ensure even cooking.
7. **Garnish and Serve:**
    - Once the vegetables are cooked to your liking and the flavors have melded together, remove the skillet from heat.
    - Garnish Ajapsandali with freshly chopped parsley or cilantro.
8. **Serve Ajapsandali:**

- Serve Ajapsandali warm as a main dish or side dish. It can be enjoyed on its own or with crusty bread, such as Georgian shotis puri or French baguette.

Tips for Making Ajapsandali:

- **Eggplants:** Salting and rinsing the eggplants before cooking helps remove bitterness and improves their texture.
- **Spices:** Adjust the amount of ground hot red pepper according to your preference for spiciness. Ground fenugreek adds a subtle, aromatic flavor to the stew.
- **Variations:** Ajapsandali can be customized with other vegetables such as zucchini, potatoes, or carrots. Adjust the cooking time accordingly for different vegetables.
- **Storage:** Leftover Ajapsandali can be stored in an airtight container in the refrigerator for up to 3 days. Reheat gently on the stove before serving.

Ajapsandali is a delicious and hearty vegetable stew that highlights the fresh flavors of seasonal vegetables and Georgian spices. It's a comforting dish that is perfect for sharing with family and friends.

Churchkhela (Georgian Candy)

Ingredients:

- 1 cup walnuts or almonds (or a mix of both)
- 1 cup grape juice or fruit juice (such as peach or apricot)
- 1 cup sugar
- 1 cup flour (optional, for thickening)

Instructions:

1. **Prepare the Nuts:**
    - Thread the walnuts or almonds onto a string or skewer, leaving space between each nut. This will allow you to dip them easily into the grape juice mixture. You can make multiple strings depending on how many Churchkhela you want to make.
2. **Make the Grape Juice Mixture:**
    - In a saucepan, combine the grape juice (or fruit juice) with sugar. Heat over medium heat, stirring occasionally, until the sugar dissolves completely.
    - Optional step: To thicken the mixture, gradually add flour while stirring constantly. Continue cooking until the mixture thickens to a syrupy consistency that coats the back of a spoon.
3. **Dip the Nuts:**
    - Once the grape juice mixture is ready, lower the heat to low to keep it warm.
    - Dip the threaded nuts into the warm grape juice mixture, ensuring they are evenly coated. Use a spoon to help coat them completely.
4. **Dry the Churchkhela:**

- Hang the coated nuts in a cool, dry place or on a drying rack to allow the excess grape juice mixture to drip off.
- Let the Churchkhela dry for about 1-2 days, depending on the humidity in your area. They should become firm and sticky to the touch.

5. **Store and Serve:**
    - Once dried, trim any excess strings and store Churchkhela in a cool, dry place in an airtight container. They can be kept for several weeks.

Tips for Making Churchkhela:

- **Nuts:** You can use any type of nuts you prefer, but walnuts and almonds are traditional choices.
- **Juice:** Traditional Churchkhela is made with grape juice, but you can also use other fruit juices like peach or apricot. The juice should be thickened slightly to ensure it coats the nuts well.
- **Thickening:** Adding flour to the juice mixture is optional. It helps thicken the coating, making it easier to handle and ensuring a more even coating on the nuts.
- **Drying:** Ensure the Churchkhela are completely dry before storing to prevent them from becoming moldy. Hang them in a well-ventilated area away from direct sunlight.

Churchkhela is a unique and delicious treat that is enjoyed in Georgia and throughout the Caucasus region. It's often eaten as a snack or dessert and is a popular souvenir item.

Lobiani (Georgian Bean-Stuffed Bread)

Ingredients:

For the Dough:

- 3 cups all-purpose flour
- 1 cup warm water
- 2 teaspoons active dry yeast
- 1 tablespoon sugar
- 1 teaspoon salt
- 2 tablespoons vegetable oil

For the Filling:

- 2 cups cooked red kidney beans (or canned beans, drained and rinsed)
- 1 onion, finely chopped
- 3 cloves garlic, minced
- 1 tablespoon vegetable oil
- 1 tablespoon ground coriander
- 1 teaspoon ground fenugreek (optional)
- 1/2 teaspoon ground hot red pepper (adjust to taste)

- Salt and pepper, to taste

For Assembly:

- All-purpose flour, for dusting
- 1 egg, beaten (for egg wash)

Instructions:

1. Prepare the Dough:

- In a small bowl, combine the warm water, sugar, and yeast. Let it sit for about 5-10 minutes until the yeast activates and becomes frothy.
- In a large mixing bowl, combine the flour and salt. Make a well in the center and pour in the yeast mixture and vegetable oil.
- Mix everything together until a dough forms. Transfer the dough to a floured surface and knead for about 5-7 minutes until smooth and elastic. Place the dough in a lightly oiled bowl, cover with a clean kitchen towel, and let it rise in a warm place for about 1-2 hours or until doubled in size.

2. Prepare the Filling:

- Heat vegetable oil in a skillet over medium heat. Add the finely chopped onion and sauté until translucent, about 5-7 minutes.
- Add the minced garlic to the skillet and sauté for another 1-2 minutes until fragrant.
- Add the cooked red kidney beans to the skillet. Mash the beans lightly with a fork or potato masher, leaving some texture.
- Stir in ground coriander, ground fenugreek (if using), ground hot red pepper (adjust to taste), salt, and pepper. Cook for another 3-5 minutes, stirring occasionally, until the flavors meld together. Remove from heat and let the filling cool slightly.

3. Assemble the Lobiani:

- Preheat your oven to 375°F (190°C). Line a baking sheet with parchment paper.
- Punch down the risen dough and divide it into equal-sized portions (about 8-10 pieces, depending on how large you want your Lobiani).
- On a floured surface, roll out each portion of dough into a circle or oval shape, about 1/4 inch thick.
- Spoon a generous amount of the bean filling onto one half of each dough circle, leaving a border around the edges.
- Fold the other half of the dough over the filling to enclose it, pressing the edges together to seal. You can crimp the edges with a fork for a decorative touch.

4. Bake the Lobiani:

- Place the assembled Lobiani on the prepared baking sheet. Brush the tops with beaten egg to give them a golden brown color when baked.
- Bake in the preheated oven for 20-25 minutes, or until the Lobiani are golden brown and cooked through.

5. Serve and Enjoy:

- Remove from the oven and let the Lobiani cool slightly on a wire rack before serving.
- Lobiani can be served warm or at room temperature. It's delicious on its own as a snack or served with a side of yogurt or a fresh salad.

Tips for Making Lobiani:

- **Bean Filling:** You can use other types of beans such as white beans or a mix of beans for the filling. Adjust the seasoning accordingly.
- **Variations:** Some recipes include adding chopped fresh herbs like cilantro or parsley to the bean filling for added flavor.
- **Storage:** Leftover Lobiani can be stored in an airtight container in the refrigerator for up to 3 days. Reheat gently in the oven or microwave before serving.

Lobiani is a wonderful example of Georgian cuisine's rich flavors and comforting dishes. It's a must-try for anyone interested in exploring traditional foods from the Caucasus region.

Badrijani Nigvzit (Georgian Eggplant Rolls)

Ingredients:

For the Eggplant Rolls:

- 2 large eggplants
- Salt, for sprinkling
- Vegetable oil, for frying

For the Walnut Filling:

- 1 cup walnuts, finely chopped or ground
- 2 cloves garlic, minced
- 1 tablespoon white wine vinegar or red wine vinegar
- 1 tablespoon pomegranate molasses (optional, for tanginess)
- 1 teaspoon ground coriander
- 1/2 teaspoon ground fenugreek (optional)
- 1/2 teaspoon ground hot red pepper (adjust to taste)
- Salt, to taste
- Fresh cilantro or parsley, finely chopped, for garnish

Instructions:

1. Prepare the Eggplants:

- Trim off the stem ends of the eggplants. Cut them lengthwise into thin slices, about 1/4 inch thick.
- Place the eggplant slices on a paper towel-lined baking sheet. Sprinkle both sides generously with salt and let them sit for about 20-30 minutes. This helps draw out bitterness from the eggplants.
- After 20-30 minutes, rinse the eggplant slices under cold water to remove the salt. Pat dry with paper towels.

2. Fry the Eggplant Slices:

- In a large skillet or frying pan, heat vegetable oil over medium heat.
- Working in batches, fry the eggplant slices until they are golden brown and tender, about 2-3 minutes per side. Transfer to a plate lined with paper towels to drain excess oil. Repeat until all eggplant slices are fried. Let them cool.

3. Make the Walnut Filling:

- In a bowl, combine finely chopped or ground walnuts with minced garlic, white wine vinegar, pomegranate molasses (if using), ground coriander, ground fenugreek (if using), ground hot red pepper, and salt. Mix well until the ingredients are thoroughly combined and the mixture holds together.

4. Assemble the Rolls:

- Take one fried eggplant slice and place a spoonful of the walnut filling at one end. Carefully roll up the eggplant slice around the filling, forming a tight roll. Repeat with the remaining eggplant slices and walnut filling.

5. Serve Badrijani Nigvzit:

- Arrange the eggplant rolls on a serving platter. Garnish with finely chopped fresh cilantro or parsley.
- Badrijani Nigvzit can be served at room temperature or chilled. It's often enjoyed as an appetizer or as part of a Georgian feast alongside other dishes like khachapuri (Georgian cheese bread) and salads.

Tips for Making Badrijani Nigvzit:

- **Walnut Filling:** Adjust the seasoning and spiciness of the walnut filling according to your taste preferences. You can also add a touch of sweetness with a little honey or sugar if desired.

- **Variations:** Some recipes include adding chopped fresh herbs like dill or mint to the walnut filling for added flavor.
- **Storage:** Badrijani Nigvzit can be stored in an airtight container in the refrigerator for up to 3 days. Bring to room temperature before serving.

Badrijani Nigvzit showcases the rich flavors and textures of Georgian cuisine, highlighting the use of nuts and spices in a unique and delicious way. It's a delightful dish to serve and enjoy with friends and family.

Satsivi (Georgian Chicken in Walnut Sauce)

Ingredients:

For the Chicken:

- 2 lbs (about 1 kg) chicken pieces (legs, thighs, or breasts)
- 1 onion, quartered
- 2 garlic cloves, crushed
- 1 bay leaf
- Salt, to taste
- Water, for boiling

For the Walnut Sauce:

- 2 cups walnuts, shelled
- 2 cups chicken broth (from boiling the chicken)
- 1 onion, finely chopped
- 4 cloves garlic, minced
- 2 tablespoons vegetable oil
- 1 tablespoon white wine vinegar or red wine vinegar
- 1 teaspoon ground coriander
- 1/2 teaspoon ground fenugreek (optional)
- 1/2 teaspoon ground hot red pepper (adjust to taste)
- Salt, to taste

For Garnish:

- Fresh cilantro or parsley, chopped
- Pomegranate seeds (optional)

Instructions:

1. Prepare the Chicken:

- In a large pot, place the chicken pieces, quartered onion, crushed garlic cloves, bay leaf, and salt. Cover with water.

- Bring to a boil over medium-high heat, then reduce the heat to low and simmer gently for about 30-40 minutes, or until the chicken is cooked through and tender. Remove the chicken from the broth and let it cool. Reserve the broth.

2. Make the Walnut Sauce:

- While the chicken is cooking, prepare the walnut sauce. In a food processor or blender, grind the walnuts until they form a fine paste, gradually adding 2 cups of the reserved chicken broth to achieve a creamy consistency.
- In a large skillet or Dutch oven, heat vegetable oil over medium heat. Add the finely chopped onion and sauté until translucent, about 5-7 minutes.
- Add the minced garlic to the skillet and sauté for another 1-2 minutes until fragrant.
- Stir in the ground coriander, ground fenugreek (if using), and ground hot red pepper. Cook for another minute to toast the spices.
- Add the walnut paste to the skillet, stirring constantly to combine with the onion and spices. Cook over medium heat for about 5-7 minutes, stirring occasionally, until the sauce thickens slightly.
- Stir in the vinegar and season with salt to taste. Simmer the sauce over low heat for another 5 minutes, stirring occasionally.

3. Combine Chicken and Walnut Sauce:

- Add the cooked chicken pieces to the skillet with the walnut sauce. Gently stir to coat the chicken pieces evenly with the sauce. Cook over low heat for another 5-10 minutes, allowing the flavors to meld together.

4. Serve Satsivi:

- Transfer the Satsivi to a serving dish. Garnish with chopped fresh cilantro or parsley, and optionally sprinkle with pomegranate seeds for a colorful presentation.
- Satsivi is traditionally served warm or at room temperature. It pairs well with Georgian bread (shotis puri) or rice.

Tips for Making Satsivi:

- **Consistency:** Adjust the thickness of the walnut sauce by adding more or less chicken broth. It should be creamy and coat the chicken pieces well.
- **Spices:** Ground fenugreek adds a unique flavor to Satsivi, but it can be omitted if unavailable. Adjust the amount of ground hot red pepper according to your preference for spiciness.
- **Storage:** Leftover Satsivi can be stored in an airtight container in the refrigerator for up to 3 days. Reheat gently on the stove before serving.

Satsivi is a delicious and comforting dish that showcases the distinctive flavors of Georgian cuisine, especially the use of walnuts in savory sauces. Enjoy this flavorful chicken dish as part of a Georgian feast or on its own with your favorite side dishes!

Chashushuli (Georgian Beef Stew)

Ingredients:

- 1 lb (450g) beef stew meat, cubed
- 2 tablespoons vegetable oil
- 2 onions, thinly sliced
- 3 cloves garlic, minced
- 2 tomatoes, chopped
- 1 red bell pepper, thinly sliced
- 1 green bell pepper, thinly sliced
- 1 tablespoon tomato paste
- 1 teaspoon ground coriander
- 1/2 teaspoon ground fenugreek (optional)
- 1/2 teaspoon hot paprika or cayenne pepper (adjust to taste)
- Salt and pepper, to taste
- Fresh parsley or cilantro, chopped, for garnish
- Cooked rice or bread, for serving

Instructions:

1. Sear the Beef:

- Heat vegetable oil in a large pot or Dutch oven over medium-high heat. Add the cubed beef stew meat and sear on all sides until browned. Remove the beef from the pot and set aside.

2. Sauté the Vegetables:

- In the same pot, add the thinly sliced onions and cook until softened and translucent, about 5-7 minutes.
- Add the minced garlic to the pot and sauté for another minute until fragrant.

3. Add Tomatoes and Spices:

- Stir in the chopped tomatoes, red bell pepper, and green bell pepper. Cook for about 5 minutes, until the vegetables begin to soften.
- Add the tomato paste, ground coriander, ground fenugreek (if using), and hot paprika or cayenne pepper. Season with salt and pepper to taste. Stir well to combine.

4. Simmer the Stew:

- Return the seared beef cubes to the pot, along with any juices that have accumulated. Stir to coat the beef and vegetables with the spices.
- Pour enough water to cover the ingredients in the pot. Bring the mixture to a boil, then reduce the heat to low. Cover the pot and simmer for 1.5 to 2 hours, or until the beef is tender and the flavors have melded together. Stir occasionally and add more water if needed to maintain a stew-like consistency.

5. Serve Chashushuli:

- Once the beef is tender and the stew has thickened to your liking, remove the pot from heat.
- Serve Chashushuli hot, garnished with chopped fresh parsley or cilantro.
- Chashushuli is traditionally enjoyed with cooked rice or Georgian bread (such as shotis puri) to soak up the flavorful sauce.

Tips for Making Chashushuli:

- **Beef:** Use beef stew meat that's suitable for slow cooking, such as chuck or round. Cut the beef into uniform cubes for even cooking.
- **Spices:** Adjust the amount of hot paprika or cayenne pepper according to your preference for spiciness. Ground fenugreek adds a unique flavor to the stew, but it can be omitted if unavailable.
- **Vegetables:** Feel free to add other vegetables like carrots or potatoes to the stew for additional texture and flavor.
- **Storage:** Chashushuli can be stored in an airtight container in the refrigerator for up to 3 days. Reheat gently on the stove before serving.

Chashushuli is a comforting and satisfying dish that showcases the robust flavors of Georgian cuisine. Enjoy this beef stew with friends and family as part of a delicious meal!

Kharcho (Georgian Beef Soup)

Ingredients:

- 1 lb (450g) beef stew meat, cubed
- 2 tablespoons vegetable oil
- 1 onion, finely chopped
- 2 cloves garlic, minced
- 2 tablespoons tomato paste
- 2 tomatoes, chopped
- 1 tablespoon ground coriander
- 1 teaspoon ground fenugreek (optional)
- 1/2 teaspoon hot paprika or cayenne pepper (adjust to taste)
- 1 cup walnuts, finely chopped or ground
- 6 cups beef broth or water

- Salt and pepper, to taste
- Fresh cilantro or parsley, chopped, for garnish
- Cooked rice, for serving

Instructions:

1. Sear the Beef:

- Heat vegetable oil in a large pot or Dutch oven over medium-high heat. Add the cubed beef stew meat and sear on all sides until browned. Remove the beef from the pot and set aside.

2. Sauté the Aromatics:

- In the same pot, add the finely chopped onion and cook until softened and translucent, about 5-7 minutes.
- Add the minced garlic to the pot and sauté for another minute until fragrant.

3. Add Tomatoes and Spices:

- Stir in the tomato paste and cook for 1-2 minutes, stirring constantly.
- Add the chopped tomatoes, ground coriander, ground fenugreek (if using), and hot paprika or cayenne pepper. Season with salt and pepper to taste. Stir well to combine.

4. Simmer the Soup:

- Return the seared beef cubes to the pot, along with any juices that have accumulated. Stir to coat the beef and vegetables with the spices.
- Pour in the beef broth or water, and bring the mixture to a boil.
- Reduce the heat to low, cover the pot, and simmer gently for about 1.5 to 2 hours, or until the beef is tender.

5. Prepare the Walnut Paste:

- While the soup is simmering, prepare the walnut paste. In a food processor or blender, grind the walnuts until they form a fine paste. You can add a little water or broth to help achieve a smooth consistency.

6. Finish the Soup:

- Once the beef is tender, stir in the walnut paste into the soup. Simmer for another 10-15 minutes, stirring occasionally, to allow the flavors to meld together.
- Taste and adjust seasoning as needed with salt and pepper.

7. Serve Kharcho:

- Ladle the hot Kharcho soup into bowls. Serve with cooked rice and garnish with chopped fresh cilantro or parsley.
- Kharcho is traditionally served hot and makes a comforting meal, especially during colder months.

Tips for Making Kharcho:

- **Walnuts:** Grind the walnuts finely to ensure they blend smoothly into the soup. The walnut paste adds richness and depth to the soup.
- **Spices:** Ground fenugreek adds a unique flavor to Kharcho, but it can be omitted if unavailable. Adjust the amount of hot paprika or cayenne pepper according to your preference for spiciness.
- **Variations:** Some recipes include adding vegetables like potatoes or carrots to the soup for additional texture and flavor.
- **Storage:** Kharcho soup can be stored in an airtight container in the refrigerator for up to 3 days. Reheat gently on the stove before serving.

Enjoy this delicious and warming Georgian beef soup, Kharcho, with its blend of savory flavors and hearty ingredients!

Jonjoli (Georgian Pickled Flowers)

Ingredients:

- 1 cup Jonjoli (pickled Bladdernut flowers), drained
- 1 small onion, thinly sliced
- 1 tablespoon fresh cilantro, chopped (optional)
- 1 tablespoon fresh parsley, chopped (optional)
- 1 tablespoon white wine vinegar or red wine vinegar
- 1 tablespoon vegetable oil
- Salt, to taste
- Ground black pepper, to taste

Instructions:

1. Prepare Jonjoli:

- Drain the Jonjoli (pickled Bladdernut flowers) from the brine. Rinse briefly under cold water if desired to reduce the saltiness, then drain well.

2. Combine Ingredients:

- In a mixing bowl, combine the drained Jonjoli with thinly sliced onion.
- Add chopped fresh cilantro and parsley (if using).
- Drizzle with white wine vinegar or red wine vinegar and vegetable oil.

3. Season and Toss:

- Season with salt and ground black pepper to taste.
- Gently toss all the ingredients together until well combined.

4. Serve Jonjoli:

- Transfer the Jonjoli salad to a serving dish or individual plates.
- Jonjoli is typically served cold or at room temperature as a side dish or appetizer.

Tips for Making Jonjoli:

- **Flavor Variations:** Some recipes may include additional ingredients such as garlic, chili flakes, or Georgian spices for added flavor.
- **Storage:** Leftover Jonjoli salad can be stored in an airtight container in the refrigerator for up to 3 days. Allow it to come to room temperature before serving again.
- **Presentation:** Garnish with additional fresh herbs or a drizzle of olive oil before serving for an extra touch of flavor and presentation.

Jonjoli is a unique and tangy delicacy that showcases the diverse flavors of Georgian cuisine. Enjoy it alongside other traditional Georgian dishes or as part of a mezze-style spread.

Kupati (Georgian Sausages)

Ingredients:

- 1 lb (450g) ground pork
- 1 lb (450g) ground beef
- 1 onion, finely chopped
- 3 cloves garlic, minced
- 1 teaspoon ground coriander
- 1 teaspoon ground fenugreek
- 1 teaspoon ground paprika
- 1 teaspoon ground cayenne pepper (adjust to taste)
- 1 teaspoon ground black pepper
- 1 teaspoon salt, or to taste
- 1/2 cup red wine vinegar
- Natural sausage casings (about 2-3 yards/meters)
- Vegetable oil, for cooking

Instructions:

1. Prepare the Sausage Casings:

- Rinse the sausage casings under cold water to remove any excess salt and soak them in warm water for about 30 minutes to soften.

2. Mix the Sausage Ingredients:

- In a large mixing bowl, combine the ground pork, ground beef, finely chopped onion, minced garlic, ground coriander, ground fenugreek, ground paprika, ground cayenne pepper, ground black pepper, salt, and red wine vinegar.
- Mix the ingredients thoroughly with your hands or a spoon until well combined and evenly distributed.

3. Stuff the Sausages:

- Carefully thread one end of the sausage casing onto a sausage stuffing funnel or a sausage maker attachment of a meat grinder.
- Stuff the sausage mixture into the casing, being careful not to overfill. Leave a little room at the end to tie a knot.
- Continue stuffing until all the mixture is used, twisting the sausage into links of desired length (typically 4-6 inches long).

4. Cook the Kupati:

- Heat a large skillet or grill pan over medium-high heat and add a drizzle of vegetable oil.
- Place the Kupati sausages in the skillet and cook for about 5-7 minutes per side, or until they are cooked through and nicely browned on the outside.
- Alternatively, you can grill the Kupati over medium-high heat on a preheated grill, turning occasionally, until fully cooked and charred slightly on the outside.

5. Serve Kupati:

- Once cooked, transfer the Kupati sausages to a serving platter.
- Serve hot with traditional Georgian sides such as tkemali sauce (plum sauce), fresh herbs, and bread.

Tips for Making Kupati:

- **Spice Adjustments:** Feel free to adjust the spices according to your taste preferences. You can also add more or less cayenne pepper for spicier or milder sausages.
- **Storage:** Uncooked Kupati sausages can be stored in the refrigerator for up to 2 days or frozen for longer storage. Thaw completely before cooking.
- **Variations:** Some recipes for Kupati may include additional ingredients such as fresh herbs like cilantro or parsley, or even grated vegetables like carrots or zucchini for added texture.

Kupati are delicious and flavorful Georgian sausages that are perfect for grilling or pan-frying. Enjoy them as part of a festive meal or as a savory snack with friends and family!

Mchadi (Georgian Cornbread)

Ingredients:

- 2 cups cornmeal (medium or coarse grind)
- 1/2 teaspoon salt
- 1 cup water (approximately)
- 1 tablespoon vegetable oil or melted butter (optional, for greasing)

Instructions:

1. Mix the Cornmeal and Salt:

- In a mixing bowl, combine the cornmeal and salt. Mix well to distribute the salt evenly throughout the cornmeal.

2. Form the Dough:

- Gradually add water to the cornmeal mixture, stirring continuously with a spoon or your hands. The goal is to achieve a thick, sticky dough consistency. Add water as needed until all the cornmeal is hydrated and the dough holds together.

3. Shape the Mchadi:

- Divide the dough into 6-8 portions, depending on how large you want your Mchadi to be.
- Wet your hands with water to prevent sticking, then take each portion of dough and shape it into a round, flat disc about 1/2 inch (1.5 cm) thick. You can also shape them into oval or rectangular shapes.

4. Cook the Mchadi:

- Heat a non-stick skillet or griddle over medium heat. You can lightly grease the skillet with vegetable oil or melted butter if desired, although traditional Mchadi is often cooked without any additional fat.
- Carefully transfer the shaped Mchadi onto the hot skillet. Cook each side for about 5-7 minutes, or until golden brown and crispy on the outside. Use a spatula to flip them halfway through cooking.
- If you prefer, you can also bake Mchadi in a preheated oven at 375°F (190°C) for about 20-25 minutes, or until they are cooked through and golden brown.

5. Serve Mchadi:

- Once cooked, transfer the Mchadi to a serving plate or basket.
- Serve warm with traditional Georgian dishes such as lobio (bean stew), satsivi (chicken in walnut sauce), or simply enjoy them with a dollop of butter or cheese.

Tips for Making Mchadi:

- **Cornmeal:** Use medium or coarse grind cornmeal for authentic texture. You can adjust the amount of water slightly depending on the absorbency of your cornmeal.
- **Flavor Variations:** Some recipes for Mchadi may include additions like grated cheese, chopped herbs (such as cilantro or parsley), or even finely chopped onions for added flavor.
- **Storage:** Mchadi are best enjoyed fresh and warm. However, you can store leftovers in an airtight container at room temperature for up to 2 days. Reheat gently in a skillet or toaster oven before serving.

Mchadi is a rustic and versatile bread that adds a delightful texture and flavor to any Georgian meal. Enjoy its crisp exterior and tender interior as a complement to various dishes or as a snack on its own.

Acharuli Khachapuri (Georgian Cheese Bread with Egg)

Ingredients:

For the Dough:

- 2 cups all-purpose flour
- 1 teaspoon active dry yeast
- 1 teaspoon sugar
- 1/2 teaspoon salt
- 3/4 cup lukewarm water
- 1 tablespoon vegetable oil

For the Filling:

- 1 cup mozzarella cheese, shredded
- 1 cup feta cheese, crumbled
- 1 egg, plus additional eggs for topping (1 per bread)
- 1 tablespoon butter, melted (for brushing)
- Salt and pepper, to taste

Instructions:

1. Prepare the Dough:

- In a small bowl, dissolve the sugar in lukewarm water. Sprinkle the yeast over the water and let it sit for about 5-10 minutes, until foamy.
- In a large mixing bowl, combine the flour and salt. Make a well in the center and pour in the yeast mixture and vegetable oil.

- Mix everything together until a dough forms. Knead the dough on a lightly floured surface for about 8-10 minutes, until it becomes smooth and elastic.
- Place the dough in a lightly oiled bowl, cover with a clean kitchen towel, and let it rise in a warm place for about 1-2 hours, or until doubled in size.

2. Prepare the Cheese Filling:

- In a mixing bowl, combine the shredded mozzarella cheese and crumbled feta cheese. Mix well and set aside.

3. Shape and Fill the Khachapuri:

- Preheat your oven to 450°F (230°C). Line a baking sheet with parchment paper.
- Divide the risen dough into two equal portions. Roll each portion into an oval shape, about 1/4 inch (0.5 cm) thick.
- Transfer each oval-shaped dough onto the prepared baking sheet.
- Fold up the edges of each oval to create a boat-like shape, with a rim around the edges.
- Divide the cheese mixture evenly between the two dough boats, spreading it out to cover the bottom of each boat.
- Crack one egg into the center of each Khachapuri boat, ensuring the egg yolk stays intact.

4. Bake the Khachapuri:

- Place the baking sheet in the preheated oven and bake for about 12-15 minutes, or until the crust is golden brown and the cheese is melted and bubbly.

5. Finish and Serve:

- Remove the Khachapuri from the oven. Brush the edges of each bread boat with melted butter.
- Season with salt and pepper to taste.
- Serve immediately while hot, allowing each person to mix the egg yolk into the melted cheese before eating.

Tips for Making Acharuli Khachapuri:

- **Cheese Options:** While mozzarella and feta are commonly used, you can also use other cheeses like sulguni, a traditional Georgian cheese, or any combination of cheeses that melt well.
- **Egg:**
    - The egg yolk should remain intact when cracking it onto the cheese filling. It will cook slightly from the residual heat of the bread once it's out of the oven.
    - For a firmer egg yolk, you can pierce it gently with a fork after baking to help it cook through a bit more.
- **Variations:**

- Some versions of Acharuli Khachapuri include adding additional toppings like cooked bacon or sautéed mushrooms.
            - Adjust the amount of cheese and egg to your preference. Some recipes use more cheese for a richer filling.
    - **Storage:** Acharuli Khachapuri is best enjoyed fresh and hot out of the oven. However, any leftovers can be stored in an airtight container in the refrigerator and reheated gently in the oven or microwave.

Acharuli Khachapuri is a delicious and indulgent Georgian dish that makes for a satisfying meal or snack. Enjoy its rich cheese filling and unique boat-like shape with friends and family!

Satsivi (Georgian Chicken in Walnut Sauce)

Ingredients:

For the Chicken:

- 2 lbs (about 1 kg) chicken thighs or chicken breasts, bone-in and skin-on
- 1 onion, chopped
- 2-3 garlic cloves, minced
- 1 bay leaf
- Salt and pepper, to taste
- Water, enough to cover the chicken

For the Walnut Sauce:

- 2 cups walnuts, shelled
- 1 onion, finely chopped
- 3 cloves garlic, minced
- 1 tablespoon ground coriander
- 1 tablespoon ground fenugreek
- 1 teaspoon ground paprika
- 1/2 teaspoon ground cinnamon
- 1/2 teaspoon ground cloves
- 1/2 teaspoon ground nutmeg
- 1/2 teaspoon cayenne pepper (optional, for heat)
- 2 cups chicken broth (from cooking chicken)
- 1/2 cup white wine vinegar or red wine vinegar
- Salt and pepper, to taste

For Garnish:

- Fresh parsley or cilantro, chopped
- Pomegranate seeds (optional)

Instructions:

1. Cook the Chicken:

- In a large pot, place the chicken pieces, chopped onion, minced garlic, bay leaf, salt, and pepper.
- Add enough water to cover the chicken. Bring to a boil over medium-high heat, then reduce the heat to low. Cover and simmer for about 30-40 minutes, or until the chicken is fully cooked and tender.
- Remove the chicken from the pot and set aside to cool. Reserve about 2 cups of the chicken broth for the walnut sauce.

2. Prepare the Walnut Sauce:

- In a food processor or blender, combine the shelled walnuts, finely chopped onion, minced garlic, ground coriander, ground fenugreek, ground paprika, ground cinnamon, ground cloves, ground nutmeg, and cayenne pepper (if using).
- Pulse or blend until you get a thick paste, gradually adding the chicken broth to thin out the sauce. You may need to scrape down the sides of the blender or processor to ensure everything is well combined.

3. Cook the Walnut Sauce:

- Transfer the walnut mixture to a large skillet or saucepan. Stir in the white wine vinegar or red wine vinegar.
- Cook over medium heat, stirring constantly, for about 10-15 minutes, or until the sauce thickens to a creamy consistency. Add more chicken broth if the sauce becomes too thick.
- Season with salt and pepper to taste. Adjust the seasoning and thickness of the sauce according to your preference.

4. Assemble the Dish:

- Once the chicken has cooled slightly, remove the skin and bones (if using bone-in chicken) and shred the meat into bite-sized pieces.
- Add the shredded chicken to the skillet with the walnut sauce. Stir gently to coat the chicken evenly with the sauce.

5. Serve Satsivi:

- Transfer the Satsivi to a serving dish or individual plates.
- Garnish with chopped fresh parsley or cilantro, and optionally sprinkle with pomegranate seeds for added color and texture.
- Serve Satsivi warm or at room temperature. It is traditionally enjoyed with Georgian bread (such as shoti or lavash) or over rice or potatoes.

Tips for Making Satsivi:

- **Walnuts:** Toasting the walnuts lightly before blending can enhance their flavor. Be careful not to over-toast as it can make them bitter.
- **Consistency:** The sauce should be thick and creamy. Adjust the amount of chicken broth to achieve the desired consistency.
- **Spices:** Feel free to adjust the amount of spices to suit your taste preferences. Satsivi traditionally has a rich blend of warm spices that complement the nutty flavor of the walnuts.
- **Storage:** Satsivi can be stored in an airtight container in the refrigerator for up to 3 days. Reheat gently on the stove, adding a splash of chicken broth to loosen the sauce if necessary.

Satsivi is a unique and delicious dish that showcases the richness of Georgian cuisine, with its creamy walnut sauce and tender chicken. Enjoy this flavorful dish for a special occasion or whenever you crave a taste of Georgia!

Pkhali (Georgian Vegetable Pâté)

Ingredients:

- 1 lb (450g) spinach (fresh or frozen)
- 1 lb (450g) beetroot (cooked and peeled)
- 1 lb (450g) carrots (cooked and peeled)
- 1 cup walnuts, finely chopped
- 3-4 garlic cloves, minced
- 1 small onion, finely chopped
- 1 tablespoon ground coriander
- 1 tablespoon ground fenugreek
- 1/2 teaspoon ground cayenne pepper (adjust to taste)
- 1/2 cup fresh cilantro, chopped
- 1/2 cup fresh parsley, chopped
- Juice of 1 lemon
- Salt and pepper, to taste
- Olive oil, for drizzling
- Pomegranate seeds, for garnish (optional)

Instructions:

1. Prepare the Vegetables:

- If using fresh spinach, wash it thoroughly. If using frozen spinach, thaw and drain excess liquid.

- Cook the beetroot and carrots until tender. You can boil or steam them until a fork easily pierces through. Allow them to cool, then peel and grate them using a grater or food processor.

2. Prepare the Walnut Mixture:

- In a food processor, combine the finely chopped walnuts, minced garlic, chopped onion, ground coriander, ground fenugreek, and ground cayenne pepper. Pulse until you get a coarse paste.

3. Mix the Vegetables and Walnut Mixture:

- In a large mixing bowl, combine the grated beetroot, grated carrots, and chopped spinach.
- Add the walnut mixture to the vegetables in the bowl.
- Add the chopped cilantro, chopped parsley, lemon juice, salt, and pepper to taste. Mix everything together thoroughly until well combined.

4. Shape and Serve Pkhali:

- Transfer the mixture to a serving dish or mold. Press it firmly to pack it down and smooth the top.
- Drizzle with olive oil and garnish with pomegranate seeds (if using) for added color and texture.
- Chill in the refrigerator for at least 1-2 hours before serving to allow the flavors to meld together.

5. Serve Pkhali:

- Once chilled, slice or scoop the Pkhali onto serving plates.
- Serve cold as an appetizer or side dish. It pairs well with Georgian bread (such as shoti or lavash) or crackers.

Tips for Making Pkhali:

- **Consistency:** The mixture should be firm enough to hold its shape when molded. If it's too wet, add more chopped walnuts or squeeze out excess liquid from the vegetables.
- **Variations:** Pkhali can be made with various vegetables such as green beans, cabbage, or even eggplant. Adjust the seasoning and spices according to your taste preferences.
- **Storage:** Pkhali can be stored in an airtight container in the refrigerator for up to 3-4 days. Allow it to come to room temperature before serving leftovers.

Pkhali is a flavorful and nutritious dish that showcases the vibrant flavors and ingredients of Georgian cuisine. Enjoy its rich taste and texture as part of a Georgian-inspired meal or as a unique appetizer for your next gathering!

Khachapuri (Georgian Cheese Bread)

Ingredients:

For the Dough:

- 3 cups all-purpose flour
- 1 teaspoon salt
- 1 teaspoon sugar
- 1 teaspoon active dry yeast
- 1 cup lukewarm milk
- 1/4 cup lukewarm water
- 2 tablespoons vegetable oil

For the Filling:

- 2 cups grated mozzarella cheese (or a combination of mozzarella and feta)
- 1 cup grated sulguni cheese (or another cheese with a similar texture and flavor)
- 1 egg, plus additional eggs for topping (1 per bread)
- 2 tablespoons butter, melted (for brushing)

Instructions:

1. Prepare the Dough:

- In a small bowl, dissolve the sugar and yeast in lukewarm water. Let it sit for about 5-10 minutes until frothy.
- In a large mixing bowl, combine the flour and salt. Make a well in the center and pour in the yeast mixture, lukewarm milk, and vegetable oil.
- Mix everything together until a dough forms. Knead the dough on a lightly floured surface for about 8-10 minutes, until it becomes smooth and elastic.
- Place the dough in a lightly oiled bowl, cover with a clean kitchen towel, and let it rise in a warm place for about 1-2 hours, or until doubled in size.

2. Prepare the Filling:

- In a mixing bowl, combine the grated mozzarella, grated sulguni (or other cheese), and 1 egg. Mix well until evenly combined. Set aside.

3. Shape and Assemble the Khachapuri:

- Preheat your oven to 450°F (230°C). Line a baking sheet with parchment paper.
- Divide the risen dough into 4 equal portions. Roll each portion into an oval or round shape, about 1/4 inch (0.5 cm) thick.
- Place a quarter of the cheese mixture in the center of each dough round, leaving a border around the edges.

- Fold up the edges of the dough to create a boat-like shape, with a rim around the edges to hold the filling.
- Crack one egg into the center of each Khachapuri boat, ensuring the egg yolk stays intact.

4. Bake the Khachapuri:

- Place the baking sheet in the preheated oven and bake for about 12-15 minutes, or until the crust is golden brown and the cheese is melted and bubbly.

5. Finish and Serve:

- Remove the Khachapuri from the oven. Brush the edges with melted butter for a shiny finish.
- Serve immediately while hot, allowing each person to mix the egg yolk into the melted cheese before eating.

Tips for Making Khachapuri:

- **Cheese Options:** Traditional Khachapuri uses sulguni cheese, but if you can't find it, you can substitute with a combination of mozzarella and feta. Adjust the ratio to your taste.
- **Egg Yolk:** For a firmer egg yolk, you can pierce it gently with a fork after baking to help it cook through a bit more.
- **Variations:** Besides Adjarian Khachapuri, there are other regional varieties such as Imeretian Khachapuri (open-faced with cheese filling) and Mingrelian Khachapuri (with extra cheese on top).
- **Storage:** Khachapuri is best enjoyed fresh and hot out of the oven. Any leftovers can be stored in an airtight container in the refrigerator and reheated gently in the oven or microwave.

Khachapuri is a beloved Georgian dish that's perfect for sharing with friends and family. Enjoy its rich cheese filling and golden, buttery crust as a delicious and comforting treat!

Khinkali (Georgian Dumplings)

Ingredients:

For the Dough:

- 2 cups all-purpose flour
- 1/2 cup lukewarm water
- 1/2 teaspoon salt

For the Filling:

- 1 lb (450g) ground beef or a mixture of beef and pork
- 1 onion, finely chopped
- 2-3 garlic cloves, minced
- 1/4 cup fresh cilantro, finely chopped
- 1/4 cup fresh parsley, finely chopped
- 1/2 teaspoon ground coriander
- 1/2 teaspoon ground cumin
- 1/2 teaspoon ground black pepper
- 1/2 teaspoon cayenne pepper (optional, for heat)
- Salt, to taste

For Cooking:

- Water, for boiling
- Salt, for seasoning the water

Instructions:

1. Prepare the Dough:

- In a large bowl, combine the flour and salt. Gradually add the lukewarm water while mixing with a spoon or your hands until a dough forms.
- Knead the dough on a lightly floured surface for about 10-15 minutes until smooth and elastic. Cover the dough with a clean kitchen towel and let it rest for at least 30 minutes.

2. Make the Filling:

- In a mixing bowl, combine the ground meat, finely chopped onion, minced garlic, chopped cilantro, chopped parsley, ground coriander, ground cumin, black pepper, cayenne pepper (if using), and salt to taste. Mix well until all ingredients are evenly distributed.

3. Shape the Khinkali:

- Divide the rested dough into small walnut-sized balls. Roll out each ball into a thin circle, about 3-4 inches (7-10 cm) in diameter.
- Place a spoonful of the meat filling (about 1-2 tablespoons) in the center of each dough circle.
- To shape the Khinkali, gather the edges of the dough circle around the filling, pleating the edges together to form a purse-like shape. Pinch and twist the top to seal tightly, leaving a small hole at the top.

4. Cook the Khinkali:

- Bring a large pot of water to a rolling boil. Season the water generously with salt.

- Carefully drop the Khinkali into the boiling water, one by one, making sure they don't stick together. Cook in batches to avoid overcrowding the pot.
- Boil the Khinkali for about 10-12 minutes, or until they float to the surface and the dough is cooked through.

5. Serve Khinkali:

- Using a slotted spoon, remove the Khinkali from the water and place them on a serving plate or tray.
- Serve hot with a side of black pepper and optionally with a spicy tomato-garlic sauce (like tkemali) or a simple yogurt sauce.

Tips for Making Khinkali:

- **Filling Variations:** Besides beef, you can use lamb, pork, or a combination of meats for the filling. Adjust the spices and seasoning accordingly.
- **Shaping Technique:** The traditional pleating technique ensures that the Khinkali hold their shape and seal well during cooking. Practice will help you perfect the pleating process.
- **Eating Khinkali:** Traditionally, Khinkali are eaten by holding them by the twisted top and taking a bite, then sipping the flavorful broth inside before eating the rest.
- **Storage:** Khinkali are best enjoyed fresh and hot. If you have leftovers, you can store them in the refrigerator for a day or two and reheat gently by steaming or pan-frying.

Khinkali are a delicious and hearty dish that reflects the rich culinary traditions of Georgia. Enjoy making these flavorful dumplings at home and share them with friends and family for a memorable dining experience!

Ostri (Georgian Beef Stew)

Ingredients:

- 1 lb (450g) beef stew meat, cut into bite-sized pieces
- 2 tablespoons vegetable oil
- 2 onions, finely chopped
- 3 garlic cloves, minced
- 2 tablespoons tomato paste
- 2 large tomatoes, diced (or 1 can diced tomatoes)
- 1 teaspoon ground coriander
- 1 teaspoon ground fenugreek
- 1 teaspoon ground paprika
- 1/2 teaspoon ground cayenne pepper (adjust to taste)
- 1 teaspoon salt, or to taste
- 1/2 teaspoon black pepper
- 2 cups beef broth or water

- Fresh cilantro or parsley, chopped (for garnish)

Instructions:

1. Brown the Beef:

- Heat the vegetable oil in a large pot or Dutch oven over medium-high heat. Add the beef stew meat in batches and brown on all sides. Remove the browned meat and set aside.

2. Sauté the Aromatics:

- In the same pot, add the chopped onions and sauté until they become translucent, about 5-7 minutes. Add the minced garlic and cook for another 1-2 minutes until fragrant.

3. Add the Tomatoes and Spices:

- Stir in the tomato paste and cook for 1-2 minutes to caramelize slightly. Add the diced tomatoes (or canned tomatoes) along with ground coriander, ground fenugreek, ground paprika, ground cayenne pepper, salt, and black pepper. Cook for another 5 minutes, stirring occasionally.

4. Simmer the Stew:

- Return the browned beef to the pot. Pour in the beef broth or water, enough to cover the meat and vegetables. Bring the mixture to a boil, then reduce the heat to low.
- Cover the pot and simmer gently for 1.5 to 2 hours, or until the beef is tender and the sauce has thickened. Stir occasionally and add more liquid if needed to maintain a stew-like consistency.

5. Serve:

- Once the Ostri is cooked and thickened to your liking, adjust the seasoning with salt and pepper if necessary.
- Serve hot, garnished with chopped fresh cilantro or parsley. Ostri pairs well with rice, mashed potatoes, or crusty bread to soak up the flavorful sauce.

Tips for Making Ostri:

- **Meat Selection:** Use stewing beef with some marbling or connective tissue, such as chuck or brisket, which becomes tender and flavorful when slow-cooked.
- **Spice Variations:** You can adjust the spices to your taste. Some variations include adding ground cinnamon or cloves for a deeper flavor profile.
- **Make Ahead:** Ostri tastes even better the next day as the flavors meld. Store leftovers in an airtight container in the refrigerator for up to 3 days or freeze for longer storage.
- **Serve with Condiments:** Offer Georgian condiments like tkemali (sour plum sauce) or adjika (spicy tomato sauce) on the side for extra flavor.

Ostri is a comforting and satisfying dish that showcases the bold flavors and culinary heritage of Georgia. Enjoy this hearty beef stew as a centerpiece for a cozy meal with friends and family!

Chashushuli (Georgian Beef Stew)

Ingredients:

- 1 lb (450g) beef stew meat, cut into bite-sized pieces
- 2 tablespoons vegetable oil
- 2 onions, finely chopped
- 3 garlic cloves, minced
- 2 large tomatoes, diced (or 1 can diced tomatoes)
- 1 bell pepper, diced
- 1 hot pepper (such as jalapeño or serrano), diced (optional, for heat)
- 1 teaspoon ground coriander
- 1 teaspoon ground paprika
- 1/2 teaspoon ground cayenne pepper (adjust to taste)
- 1 teaspoon salt, or to taste
- 1/2 teaspoon black pepper
- 1 cup beef broth or water
- Fresh cilantro or parsley, chopped (for garnish)

Instructions:

1. Brown the Beef:

- Heat the vegetable oil in a large pot or Dutch oven over medium-high heat. Add the beef stew meat in batches and brown on all sides. Remove the browned meat and set aside.

2. Sauté the Aromatics:

- In the same pot, add the chopped onions and sauté until they become translucent, about 5-7 minutes. Add the minced garlic and cook for another 1-2 minutes until fragrant.

3. Add Tomatoes and Peppers:

- Stir in the diced tomatoes, bell pepper, and hot pepper (if using). Cook for about 5 minutes, stirring occasionally, until the vegetables start to soften.

4. Season the Stew:

- Return the browned beef to the pot. Add ground coriander, ground paprika, ground cayenne pepper, salt, and black pepper. Mix well to coat the meat and vegetables with the spices.

5. Simmer the Stew:

- Pour in the beef broth or water, enough to cover the meat and vegetables. Bring the mixture to a boil, then reduce the heat to low.
- Cover the pot and simmer gently for 1.5 to 2 hours, or until the beef is tender and the sauce has thickened. Stir occasionally and add more liquid if needed to maintain a stew-like consistency.

6. Serve:

- Once the Chashushuli is cooked and the sauce has thickened to your liking, adjust the seasoning with salt and pepper if necessary.
- Serve hot, garnished with chopped fresh cilantro or parsley. Chashushuli is traditionally enjoyed with crusty bread, rice, or mashed potatoes.

Tips for Making Chashushuli:

- **Meat Selection:** Use beef stew meat that has some marbling or connective tissue, such as chuck or brisket, which becomes tender and flavorful when slow-cooked.
- **Spice Variations:** Feel free to adjust the spices to your taste. Some variations include adding ground cinnamon or cloves for a deeper flavor profile.
- **Make Ahead:** Like many stews, Chashushuli tastes even better the next day as the flavors meld. Store leftovers in an airtight container in the refrigerator for up to 3 days or freeze for longer storage.
- **Serve with Condiments:** Offer Georgian condiments like tkemali (sour plum sauce) or adjika (spicy tomato sauce) on the side for extra flavor.

Chashushuli is a comforting and satisfying dish that showcases the bold flavors and culinary heritage of Georgia. Enjoy this hearty beef stew as a centerpiece for a cozy meal with friends and family!

Khinkali (Georgian Dumplings)

Ingredients:

For the Dough:

- 2 cups all-purpose flour
- 1/2 cup lukewarm water
- 1/2 teaspoon salt

For the Filling:

- 1 lb (450g) ground beef or a mixture of beef and pork
- 1 onion, finely chopped
- 2-3 garlic cloves, minced
- 1/4 cup fresh cilantro, finely chopped

- 1/4 cup fresh parsley, finely chopped
- 1/2 teaspoon ground coriander
- 1/2 teaspoon ground cumin
- 1/2 teaspoon ground black pepper
- 1/2 teaspoon cayenne pepper (optional, for heat)
- Salt, to taste

For Cooking:

- Water, for boiling
- Salt, for seasoning the water

Instructions:

1. Prepare the Dough:

- In a large bowl, combine the flour and salt. Gradually add the lukewarm water while mixing with a spoon or your hands until a dough forms.
- Knead the dough on a lightly floured surface for about 10-15 minutes until smooth and elastic. Cover the dough with a clean kitchen towel and let it rest for at least 30 minutes.

2. Make the Filling:

- In a mixing bowl, combine the ground meat, finely chopped onion, minced garlic, chopped cilantro, chopped parsley, ground coriander, ground cumin, black pepper, cayenne pepper (if using), and salt to taste. Mix well until all ingredients are evenly distributed.

3. Shape the Khinkali:

- Divide the rested dough into small walnut-sized balls. Roll out each ball into a thin circle, about 3-4 inches (7-10 cm) in diameter.
- Place a spoonful of the meat filling (about 1-2 tablespoons) in the center of each dough circle.
- To shape the Khinkali, gather the edges of the dough circle around the filling, pleating the edges together to form a purse-like shape. Pinch and twist the top to seal tightly, leaving a small hole at the top.

4. Cook the Khinkali:

- Bring a large pot of water to a rolling boil. Season the water generously with salt.
- Carefully drop the Khinkali into the boiling water, one by one, making sure they don't stick together. Cook in batches to avoid overcrowding the pot.
- Boil the Khinkali for about 10-12 minutes, or until they float to the surface and the dough is cooked through.

5. Serve Khinkali:

- Using a slotted spoon, remove the Khinkali from the water and place them on a serving plate or tray.
- Serve hot with a side of black pepper and optionally with a spicy tomato-garlic sauce (like tkemali) or a simple yogurt sauce.

Tips for Making Khinkali:

- **Filling Variations:** Besides beef, you can use lamb, pork, or a combination of meats for the filling. Adjust the spices and seasoning accordingly.
- **Shaping Technique:** The traditional pleating technique ensures that the Khinkali hold their shape and seal well during cooking. Practice will help you perfect the pleating process.
- **Eating Khinkali:** Traditionally, Khinkali are eaten by holding them by the twisted top and taking a bite, then sipping the flavorful broth inside before eating the rest.
- **Storage:** Khinkali are best enjoyed fresh and hot. If you have leftovers, you can store them in the refrigerator for a day or two and reheat gently by steaming or pan-frying.

Khinkali are a delicious and hearty dish that reflects the rich culinary traditions of Georgia. Enjoy making these flavorful dumplings at home and share them with friends and family for a memorable dining experience!

Lobio (Georgian Bean Stew)

Ingredients:

- 2 cups red kidney beans, dried (or 4 cups canned kidney beans, drained and rinsed)
- 1 large onion, finely chopped
- 3 garlic cloves, minced
- 2 tablespoons vegetable oil
- 2 tablespoons tomato paste
- 2 tomatoes, diced (or 1 can diced tomatoes)
- 1 teaspoon ground coriander
- 1 teaspoon ground fenugreek (optional)
- 1 teaspoon ground paprika
- 1/2 teaspoon ground cayenne pepper (adjust to taste)
- 1 bay leaf
- Salt and pepper, to taste
- Fresh cilantro or parsley, chopped (for garnish)

Instructions:

1. Prepare the Beans:

- If using dried kidney beans, soak them in water overnight. Drain and rinse the beans thoroughly.
- In a large pot, cover the soaked beans with fresh water. Bring to a boil, then reduce the heat and simmer for 1-1.5 hours, or until the beans are tender. Alternatively, you can use a pressure cooker to cook the beans more quickly.

2. Cook the Onion and Garlic:

- In a separate large pot or Dutch oven, heat the vegetable oil over medium heat. Add the chopped onion and sauté until it becomes translucent, about 5-7 minutes. Add the minced garlic and cook for another minute until fragrant.

3. Add Tomato Paste and Spices:

- Stir in the tomato paste and cook for 1-2 minutes to caramelize slightly. Add the diced tomatoes (or canned tomatoes) along with ground coriander, ground fenugreek (if using), ground paprika, ground cayenne pepper, bay leaf, salt, and pepper. Mix well to combine.

4. Combine with Beans:

- Add the cooked kidney beans (either drained from cooking water or rinsed if using canned beans) to the pot with the tomato and spice mixture. Stir gently to combine all ingredients.

5. Simmer the Stew:

- Bring the mixture to a boil, then reduce the heat to low. Cover the pot and simmer gently for about 20-30 minutes to allow the flavors to meld together. Stir occasionally and add a splash of water if the stew becomes too thick.

6. Serve:

- Once the Lobio is cooked and the flavors have developed, adjust the seasoning with salt and pepper if necessary.
- Serve hot, garnished with chopped fresh cilantro or parsley. Lobio is traditionally enjoyed with crusty bread, rice, or as a side dish to complement other Georgian dishes.

Tips for Making Lobio:

- **Variations:** You can add more vegetables such as bell peppers or carrots for additional flavor and texture.
- **Spice Level:** Adjust the amount of cayenne pepper based on your preference for spiciness.
- **Storage:** Lobio can be stored in an airtight container in the refrigerator for up to 3 days. Reheat gently on the stove with a splash of water or broth to maintain its consistency.

Lobio is a comforting and nutritious dish that highlights the rich culinary heritage of Georgia. Enjoy making this flavorful bean stew at home and share it with family and friends for a taste of Georgian cuisine!

Ajapsandali

Ingredients:

- 2 medium eggplants
- 2 large potatoes
- 2 onions, finely chopped
- 3 garlic cloves, minced
- 4 ripe tomatoes, diced (or 1 can diced tomatoes)
- 1 bell pepper, diced
- 1 hot pepper (such as jalapeño or serrano), diced (optional, for heat)
- 1 teaspoon ground coriander
- 1 teaspoon ground paprika
- 1/2 teaspoon ground cayenne pepper (adjust to taste)
- Salt and pepper, to taste
- Fresh cilantro or parsley, chopped, for garnish
- Vegetable oil, for cooking

Instructions:

1. Prepare the Vegetables:

- Peel the eggplants and potatoes (if desired). Cut them into medium-sized cubes.

2. Sauté the Onions and Garlic:

- Heat a couple of tablespoons of vegetable oil in a large pot or Dutch oven over medium heat. Add the finely chopped onions and sauté until they become translucent, about 5-7 minutes. Add the minced garlic and cook for another minute until fragrant.

3. Add Tomatoes and Spices:

- Stir in the diced tomatoes, bell pepper, and hot pepper (if using). Cook for about 5 minutes, stirring occasionally, until the vegetables start to soften.
- Add ground coriander, ground paprika, ground cayenne pepper, salt, and pepper to the pot. Mix well to combine with the vegetables.

4. Cook the Vegetables:

- Add the cubed eggplants and potatoes to the pot. Gently stir to coat the vegetables with the tomato and spice mixture.
- Cover the pot and cook over low to medium heat for about 30-40 minutes, stirring occasionally, until the eggplants and potatoes are tender and cooked through. If the mixture becomes too dry, add a splash of water to prevent sticking.

5. Serve Ajapsandali:

- Once the vegetables are cooked to your desired tenderness and the flavors have melded together, adjust the seasoning with salt and pepper if necessary.
- Serve Ajapsandali warm or at room temperature, garnished with chopped fresh cilantro or parsley.

Tips for Making Ajapsandali:

- **Variations:** Some versions of Ajapsandali include zucchini or carrots for added texture and flavor.
- **Spice Level:** Adjust the amount of cayenne pepper based on your preference for spiciness.
- **Storage:** Ajapsandali can be stored in an airtight container in the refrigerator for up to 3 days. Reheat gently on the stove or in the microwave before serving.

Ajapsandali is a delightful dish that showcases the fresh flavors of vegetables and the aromatic spices typical of Georgian cuisine. Enjoy this vegetarian stew as a main course or as a side dish with bread or rice for a complete meal!